T0110160

SEEKERS
of
TRUTH

Psalms and Prayers for
Our World Today

REBECCA B. MULLICAN

WESTBOW
PRESS®
A DIVISION OF THOMAS NELSON
& ZONDERVAN

Copyright © 2020 Rebecca B. Mullican.

All rights reserved. No part of this book may be used or reproduced by any means, graphic, electronic, or mechanical, including photocopying, recording, taping or by any information storage retrieval system without the written permission of the author except in the case of brief quotations embodied in critical articles and reviews.

This book is a work of non-fiction. Unless otherwise noted, the author and the publisher make no explicit guarantees as to the accuracy of the information contained in this book and in some cases, names of people and places have been altered to protect their privacy.

WestBow Press books may be ordered through booksellers or by contacting:

WestBow Press
A Division of Thomas Nelson & Zondervan
1663 Liberty Drive
Bloomington, IN 47403
www.westbowpress.com
1 (866) 928-1240

Because of the dynamic nature of the Internet, any web addresses or links contained in this book may have changed since publication and may no longer be valid. The views expressed in this work are solely those of the author and do not necessarily reflect the views of the publisher, and the publisher hereby disclaims any responsibility for them.

Any people depicted in stock imagery provided by Getty Images are models, and such images are being used for illustrative purposes only.
Certain stock imagery © Getty Images.

NKJV: Scripture taken from the New King James Version® Copyright © 1982 by Thomas Nelson. Used by permission. All rights reserved.

NIV: Scripture quotations taken from The Holy Bible, New International Version® NIV® Copyright © 1973 1978 1984 2011 by Biblica, Inc. TM. Used by permission. All rights reserved worldwide.

KJV: Scripture taken from the King James Version of the Bible.

ESV: "Scripture quotations are from the ESV® Bible (The Holy Bible, English Standard Version®), copyright © 2001 by Crossway, a publishing ministry of Good News Publishers. Used by permission. All rights reserved."

MSV: "The Book of Enoch quotations are from the MSV™ (The Book of Enoch, Modern Standard Version™), copyright © 2017 by Kip Farrar. Used by permission. All rights reserved."

ISBN: 978-1-9736-9746-6 (sc)
ISBN: 978-1-9736-9748-0 (hc)
ISBN: 978-1-9736-9747-3 (e)

Library of Congress Control Number: 2020913190

Print information available on the last page.

WestBow Press rev. date: 7/27/2020

Introduction

First time author Rebecca Burgin Mullican gives insights for how to remain strong and secure in your Christian walk during these uncertain times in her book **Seekers of Truth, Psalms and Prayers for Our Modern World**. Original psalms and prayers, from the author's own experiences, those of family and friends and prompting of the Holy Spirit, deal with emotions, circumstances, attitudes, trials and heartaches people of faith are facing today. As Christianity is being maligned and made fun of, we need encouragement and support to stand firm and realize that we are not alone. This book will give comfort and strength to those seeking to know and live the true path of righteousness. Readers will see that God is everything and anything we need no matter what the frustrations and pitfalls we experience every day. Delving into the Christians struggle to live as Jesus taught us, these psalms will impart a deeper knowledge and understanding of who God is and how He is working for us. As the enemy assaults our mind, body and emotions, with all the temptations the modern world brings, we can find it very hard to find peace and joy in our lives. Disappointments trials and heartaches are common circumstances among believers today. **Seekers of Truth** is a source of hope and encouragement for living lives of joy and peace in all things. Written in contemporary language and using common everyday circumstances, readers will find themselves on many pages of this book. They will find joy for the disheartened, hope for the broken, solace for the sorrowing and more truths for those living in our world today. Readers will also find psalms and prayers for family, children, love, and other things which bring us joy. Warnings for our country and our world are also included from the Word of God. This book is an inspirational must read for all people of faith and anyone who is asking,

"What in the world is going on and how can we continue to live in this broken world?"

This book can be read straight through or used as a daily devotional. Readers can look up a Psalm or Prayer for their need by referencing the table of contents,

Preface

What in the world is going on? That is a question I ask myself every day. Our society seems to have turned to evil. Murder, riots, looting, bigotry, and hatred have consumed our once peaceful nation. People who strive to live godly lives are suffering persecution that is getting worse. How do we cope? How do we rest? How do we continue to live lives of holiness?

I started writing this book several years ago with no awareness of what was going to be happening today, but I knew that God was prompting my heart to do something that might help others in difficult times. As I look back on my life, I realize that I have been through some circumstances that might offer others hope. As I prayed about what to do, the Holy Spirit began pouring words and feelings into my soul to share with others.

Throughout my life, there have been many times when I felt there was no hope, and I could find no peace. I could not understand why certain things were happening. I was mad and disappointed in God. It took much prayer and study to help me realize that God is the only source of peace, comfort, hope, and joy. l must depend on God in every time, in every place, and in every circumstance.

As I studied the Scriptures more deeply, I began to understand the nature of God and how He loves us and wants us to depend on Him and His Word above anything in this world. He can give us hope amid the evil surrounding us today, no matter what is going on around us.

During the writing of this book, I experienced circumstances that affected me greatly. The death of my Dad, becoming a caregiver for my husband, debilitating physical pain, and addiction in my family are only a few. These experiences, which taught me how to keep hope, enriched my faith, and I share them believing they will do the same for you. Throughout the pages of this book, I reveal my heartbreak over abortion, child abuse, perversion, and hate along with warnings that God gives us in His Word about our future.

I have learned that praise and prayer are powerful tools to allow God to act. I have also learned about the responsibility we have to God and ourselves, and that no matter the circumstance, God is with us. We must trust in Him completely. I pray that the lessons reflected in this book will be an inspiration and a source of hope to all readers. The Holy Scriptures and the Holy Spirit gave me the words to write.

I want to thank my mother, who has been a constant source of encouragement and support and who kept me going when I was ready to quit. Thanks to my husband for graciously helping with the mundane things so that I would have time to pray and write. I also thank my dear friend and editor, Linda Towson Yawn, for taking my rough form and polishing it to perfection.

Contents

SECTION 1   PSALMS OF PRAISE.. 1

- Psalm of Praise.. 4
- Psalm of Praise 2... 5
- Psalm of Praise 3... 6
- Psalm of Longing... 8
- Psalm of Worship 9
- Psalm of Singing..11
- Psalm of Exaltation to God.. 13
- Psalm of Praise 4...15

SECTION 2   PSALMS OF GOD'S NATURE 17

- Psalm to the King of Kings.. 22
- Psalm to the Great I Am.. 24
- Psalm of Our Savior's Gifts... 26
- Psalm to the God of All.. 28
- Psalm to the Bigness of God 29
- Psalm of God's Faithfulness.. 32
- Psalm of Our Messiah 34
- Psalm of the Works of the Holy Spirit 39
- Psalm to the Blood of Jesus... 42
- Psalm to the Almighty.. 44

SECTION 3   PSALMS OF CREATION 49

- Psalm of Nature... 53
- Psalm of Reflections on a Day at the Beach 56
- Psalm of Two Adams... 59
- Psalm of My True Destiny... 63
- Psalm of Shells.. 65

SECTION 4   PSALMS FOR CHILDREN AND FAMILIES......... 69

- Psalm for Children 74
- Psalm to Parents 77
- Psalm of My Legacy 80
- Psalm of Heroes and Princesses.. 82
- Psalm of Prayer of the Caregiver 85
- Psalm of Prayer for My Grandchildren 88
- Psalm on the Death of a Spouse... 92
- Psalm of Letting Go 94

SECTION 5   PSALMS OF GOD'S PRESENCE AND
            ENCOURAGEMENT.. 97

- Psalm of Battle 100
- Psalm of Security.. 101
- Psalm of Our Savior's Plea 103
- Psalm of War 104
- Psalm of God's Word.. 106
- Psalm of God's Love 108
- Psalm of Man 110

SECTION 6   PSALMS FOR DOUBT AND BROKENESS 113

- A Psalm of Addiction... 118
- Psalm of Desolation.. 121
- Psalm for the Sick 122
- Psalm of Darkness 124

- Psalm of Prayer for Pain 126
- Psalm of Life's Disappointments 128
- Psalm of Prayer For Redemption 132
- Psalm of Fear 137
- Psalm of My Life 140
- Psalm of Doubt 144

SECTION 7   PSALMS OF LIVING IN CHRIST 147

- Psalm of Living 151
- Psalm of Mission 152
- Psalm of Obedience 154
- Psalm on Micah 6: 8 157
- Psalm on The Fruit of The Spirit 159
- Psalm of God's First Command 161
- Psalm of Discouragement 163
- Psalm of Things I Have Learned in My Life 165
- Psalm of Promises 169
- Psalm of The Power of Words 173
- Psalm of Choice 177
- Psalm of Time 179
- Psalm of Courage 182
- Psalm of Assurance 184
- Psalm of Forgiveness 187

SECTION 8   PSALMS OF PRAYER 193

- Psalm of Call to Prayer (We Need to Be on Our Knees) 198
- Psalm of Prayer for Forgiveness 201
- Psalm of Prayer for Intervention (Psalm of a Virus) 204
- Psalm of Prayer 208
- Psalm of Prayer for Salvation 211
- Psalm of Prayer on Maundy Thursday 213

SECTION 9   PSALMS OF WARNING 215

- Psalm of Warning.. 220
- Psalm of Darkness and Light 224
- Psalm of Sorrow.. 226
- Psalm of the Gods of this World............................ 229
- Psalm of Heaven and Hell 233

SECTION 10 PSALMS OF VICTORY 237

- Psalm of Release 242
- Psalm to Death.. 244
- A Psalm for the Church in the Modern Age 246

SECTION 1

PSALMS OF PRAISE

Psalm to the Lord

To the Lord God Almighty, reigning in heavenly splendor,
I lift my hands in joyful praise and adoration.
Your majesty shines brighter than the sun.
Your mercy reaches beyond the widest sea.

Your great love extends from east to west.
Your grace reaches out to every living being.
Your eyes see each heart and measure its devotion,
And Your judgment is swift on those who reject You.

You have given Your word, O Lord, for instruction.
It is good, it is true, and it is pure.
My heart and mind search to know its depths
As I seek Your will for my life.

Your Holiness is too great for my mind to comprehend.
Your face shines with the glory of a million suns.
Your power and Your might are demonstrated in all the universe.
Yet, Your amazing love You offer to all.

My Lord and my God, how can it be
That You would turn from Your mighty
throne to look on one such as me?
I am not worthy of the gifts that You give,
But You made me the daughter of the Almighty King.

I praise You O God, Lord of the ages,
Creator, Redeemer, Savior, and King.
I will proclaim Your greatness to the heavens
And lift my hands in praise to You.

Psalm of Praise

I do not understand the power that can take this life I live
And turn it into something good, strong, and true.
I do not know how you could love me when I strive against your will,
But I know that it can only come from You.

I do not know if I can ever comprehend the things You do
To fill my life up with Your Spirit and Your love.
I do not know how I can thank You for Your touch that set me free.
I only know that I must raise my voice to You.

For You are God, and Your love is full of holiness.
You are God, and Your light is full of changing power.
You are God, and Your Hand pours forth redeeming grace.
You are God, Almighty God, forever more.

God of heaven, God of earth, God of creation--
God of everything that was and is to come.
God of glory, God of might and restoration,
God of life and death and of the empty tomb.

You are God, and Your hand is full of miracles.
You are God, and Your heart is full of loving grace.
You are God, and Your might is there protecting me.
Yes, You are God, Almighty God forevermore.

Psalm of Praise 2

The Lord God Almighty reigns.
Praise the name of the Lord.
Omnipotent Father, Glorious King,
Praise His name, all the earth.

From beginning to end, He rules from on high.
His glory shines over His children.
He reigns on His throne in merciful might--
Praise the Lord; Praise His name.

It is only in praise we may come
To enter the presence of God.
His gates open wide at the sound of our tongues
As we praise His name.

Glory and honor, thanksgiving and laud
Allow us to enter His throne room.
His blessings flow out as we lift our voices
In praise to Him.

The Lord, God Almighty reigns.
Praise the name of the Lord.
Omnipotent Father, glorious King,
Praise His name, all the earth.

Psalm of Praise 3

How can I worship you high enough
With my simple words that are inadequate?
How do I honor You great enough
With the smallness of my understanding?

Almighty God, King of Heaven, Lord of All,
I speak and I sing Your greatness.
My voice and my hands I raise high in praise
To proclaim my love for You.

King of Glory, my mind cannot comprehend
The brightness and goodness of Your presence.
My eyes cannot look on the glory
Or the essence of Your beauty and grace.

Godhead, three in one, supreme being,
I can hardly comprehend the thought.
In my limited mind I struggle
To see who You really are.

Lamb of God, Messiah, Emmanuel--
The one who gave me salvation.
To bring me from darkness to light,
You gave up Your life for my sins.

Man of sorrows, they called You in the garden.[1]
And when You suffered and bled on the cross,
With cries reaching out to the heavens
Are beyond my ability to grasp.

My perception of You is so lacking.
I struggle to know what to say.
I am so small in comparison to You.
My simple words are insufficient.

Lover of my soul, I know that You are,
And Your love is so beautifully perfect.
There is nothing I can say or do
That is conditional for Your love.

The truth, the life, the way,[2]
All names beyond comprehension.
The totality of You is a mystery;
One so supernatural I cannot conceive it.

But in my feeble voice,
In my limited view,
I know beyond a doubt
That my life belongs to You.

So, I will continue to praise You
Even though I feel insignificant.
I know that You see my heart,
And know my love for You.

I praise You for the knowledge
That You hear my humble voice.
You raise me up, as I praise You,
To the foot of Your precious throne.

Give me the words to extol You
With the glory You deserve.
I submit my voice to You, Lord,
To honor Your Holy Name.

Psalm of Longing

O Lord most Holy, Lord God Almighty,
We long to know Your power and Your might.
Forever praise we, our lips exalt thee
As we seek to know Your presence and Your light.

We yearn to see Your power as in the days of old.
We cry to hear Your voice speak to us.
We seek to see the willing of your heart unfold.
Come pour on us Your sacred trust.

How great You are.
How wonderful Your name.
How great You are.
Your power we proclaim.

Psalm of Worship

Great are you, Lord, and greatly to be praised,[3]
We honor Your holy name.
We lift our voices in song to You,
And our hands we lift in praise.

For You are the Creator of heaven and earth.
You hung the sun and moon in space.
You breathed Your own breath into man.
In Your likeness we exist in this place.

We see Your creation with wonder and awe,
Each detail You set into place.
That we might enjoy the beauty of the earth
And know of Your love and Your grace.

Your wisdom and knowledge exceed our finite minds.
You see beyond what we can imagine.
Yet, You gave us this world so beautiful and rich,
And You trust us with Your creation.

You give us everything we need
Even when we do not deserve it.
Your love to us reaches the utmost heights.
Your provision is everlasting.

When our world deserves Your anger and wrath,
When our sins we flaunt in Your face,
You offer salvation to each person on earth
By the blood of Jesus the Christ.

How great are you Lord, how compassionate and loving.
Even as You see us move away from You,
Your voice calls us back from a world full of darkness
To come live in the light You exude.

Our praises and thanks we offer to You.
We will not forget Your mercy.
No matter how far we may stray from Your love,
You welcome us back with forgiveness.

O wondrous God, our Father and Maker,
Pour out Your Spirit on us.
Let us never forget the things You have done
To draw us into Your fold.

Great are You, Lord, and greatly to be praised.
In majesty and power You reign.
God of heaven, God of earth, and God of mankind,
All praise and thanksgiving we raise.

Psalm of Singing

Sing to the Lord, all ye lands.
Lift your voices in adulation to the King.
Sing from the depths of your heart
In honor and glory to Him.

Sing with joy and admiration
To the Lord who gives us life.
Sing in worship to His name
For He is the King of Kings.

Sing with the trumpet and horn
And with instruments of strings.
Sing with the tambourine and drums.
Make a joyful noise to Him.

Sing with songs of praise.
Sing songs of His glory and righteousness.
Sing hymns of His wonder and might.
Sing in chorus with the children of God.

Sing hallelujah to the Lord on high.
Lift your voice in eternal thanksgiving.
Exalt Him for His goodness and mercy
And for all the blessings of life.

Sing songs of gratitude to the Christ.
Raise your voice, your hands, and your heart.
Ascribe to Him songs of blessing--
He deserves our thanks and our praise.

Sing in times of happiness.
Sing through times of sorrow.
Sing even when your heart is heavy.
Sing with praise in all things.

Sing loudly to proclaim His greatness.
Sing softly in worship and awe.
Sing from the depths of your being
To acknowledge your love for Him.

Open the gates of heaven with song.
Approach the throne of glory with praise.
God rejoices in our songs to Him.
He loves the sound of our worship.

Psalm of Exaltation to God

Beautiful, precious Savior,
I pour out my praise to You.
Honor, laud, and glory I give--
You alone deserve highest acclaim.

You are gracious, tender, and gentle,
Yet, You are worthy to judge all nations.
Your love is full of compassion.
Yet, Your anger will not be silent forever.

Your glory shines brightly from Your throne--
So bright I cannot look upon it,
But You allow me into Your presence
Through prayer and supplication.

Wondrous and magnificent are You,
King of all heaven and earth.
Creator and maker of all I behold,
To Your wisdom and knowledge, I bow.

I exalt Your Name, O Lord,
It embodies everything You are.
There is no true God but You,
Forever was and is and will be.

I praise You for Your faithfulness.
My needs are always provided.
Your love will never forsake me,
No matter how far I stray.

I magnify Your majesty,
With my voice I lift Your name.
My hands and my heart I give to You
In surrender and praise to Your greatness.

I will never cease to glorify You
Though my words cannot do You justice.
From my heart and my soul comes my deepest love
For You my Savior and Lord.

Psalm of Praise 4

Lord most high, praise be to You.
Praise rises from Your creation.
The rocks and the mountains extol Your name,
All things bow to Your greatness.

How mighty and strong is Your power!
Your Hand rules the universe.
The King of Glory reigns in holiness;
Every creature bows in reverence.

Your faithfulness to Your creation
Is made evident in all the earth.
The seasons turn in order
To mark birth and death and rebirth.

How vast and infinite is Your wisdom.
It has been so from the beginning.
Every detail of Your creation
Points to Your all-knowing Hand.

The sun, the moon, and the stars,
Reflect the brightness of Your glory.
The workings of the universe
Display the mysteries of Your power.

Yet, man, Your crowning creation,
Pulls away in self-righteousness.
The praise You deserve from mankind
Is dampened by sins of the world.

Great God, who is hailed by nature
As Creator and maker of all,
Forgive Your people of sin and pride.
Restore our devotion to You.

Let us lift our voice in adoration
To the one who gave us life.
He knit us together before we were born
To be a people of His own heart.

God of might, God of mercy, God of love,
You deserve our honor and praise.
As with nature and all Your creation,
We sing the glory of Your name.

SECTION 2

PSALMS OF GOD'S NATURE

Psalm of God's Name

The name of the Lord be praised.
Lift it up for honor and glory.
His name reveals the depth of His reach,
His knowledge, His love, and His power.

"I Am" is the only true God![4]
There is none greater in glory.
Omniscient, Omnipotent, Holy God,
The one who deserves our worship.

Elohim is the God of creation,
Whose hand carved the substance of life.
Jehovah is the Lord of the world,
Who has stood from the beginning of time.

Adonai is my Lord and Master,
The lover of my soul
He is my forever Father,
Who holds me close as His own.

So many names describe Him.
They all tell of his greatness and love.
No one name is sufficient
To describe the completeness of God.

Jehovah-Rohi is my shepherd,
The living one who sees me.
He numbers the hairs on my head
And keeps me in His fold.

His provision is promised forever.
Jehovah-Jireh is His name.
I shall not want for anything.
He already knows my need.

Peace He gives to my soul.
He makes me lie down unafraid.
Jehovah-Shalom will be with me
In all of life's threatening storms.

Jehovah-Rophe is my healer;
The great physician is He.
He restores my soul and refreshes my mind,
And my body He cares for as well.

The Lord is my righteousness;
Jehovah-Tsidkenu is His name.
He speaks to me in the depths of temptation
And removes the guilt from my soul.

My banner, my conqueror, my victory
For courage that defeats all foes.
Jehovah- Nissi will prevail.
No evil will befall my soul.

It is such a comfort to know
That my God is always here.
God's presence guards my way.
Jehovah- Shammah is His Name.

Jehovah-M'Kaddesh sanctifies me.
By His name I can now dwell in His presence.
He allows me to enter His throne room
Knowing my sins are forgiven.

El Shaddai is Almighty God,
The one who supplies all my needs.
He is the all sufficient one.
In trouble His strength sustains.

The Lord of Hosts is my defender.
Jehovah Sabaoth is His Name.
He sends me heavenly protection and aid.
His angels fight in my battles.

Messiah gave His life for my own.
He brings me salvation and love.
He poured out His blood to save my soul
That I may dwell in His house forever.

Mere names and words are not nearly enough,
His glory and mercy to tell.
My mind can only see dimly
The glory ascribed to Him.

There is not a page that is long enough
To contain a description of God.
The angels above praise Him continuously.
Yet, they can never praise Him enough.

How can a person so frail as I
Ever imagine the true name that is God?
My words are only a feeble attempt
To praise and honor who He is.

One day my eyes will be opened.
I will behold Him in all His glory.
I will know him completely and finally
And join the angels in singing His name.

Psalm to the King of Kings

Mighty Warrior, King of the earth,
We lift our hands to You.
We sing Your praise in adoration and honor.
To You our voices we raise.

In every circumstance, we praise You.
In joy and in sorrow, we thank You.
In days of want, we will trust You.
For provision is in Your hand.

Our enemies we do not fear.
They will be trampled to dust by Your might.
Though we see trouble on every hand,
We will trust in Your promise to fight.

We see our brothers crushed by the sword;
The sorrow goes deep in our hearts.
We see persecution everywhere,
And we struggle to remember Your Word.

You are victorious, O Lord on high.
You will carry us in Your hand.
We rest securely under Your wings,
As You crush the enemy under Your heel.

There is no enemy, no demon, or power
Sent by the evil one
Who can stand against, and destroy Your people
When we rest in the palm of Your hand.

We praise Your greatness and promise
To never let go of Your people.
Though we may be discouraged,
You provide a place of rest.

How gracious You are to Your children.
We trust and believe Your Word.
We will stand fast in the day of evil
With the mighty sword of the Spirit.

You promised never to forsake us
No matter what our earthly eyes see.
Your Spirit resides within us
To give us the victory.

Great and powerful, Warrior King,
We will praise You continually
With lifted hands and trusting heart.
We stand on Your Word to us.

Psalm to the Great I Am

Who is the King of Glory?[5]
The strong and Almighty God.
Who is the great Creator?
The Master of all the earth.

He is the Great "I Am,[6]"
The way, the truth, the light.
There is no darkness or fear.
His presence is full of light.

He is the bread of life.
In Him we will never hunger.
For righteousness and eternal life,
He gave with His own sacrifice.

The Good Shepherd of all is He.
He always abides with His flock.
Protection, provision, and presence--
In Him we find rest for our soul.

The light of all the world,
Shining in glory and honor,
Was born in a manger so lowly
To bring us all to salvation.

He is the vine on which we grow
To become His branches of peace.
We are His hands and feet on earth,
To bear the fruit of His Spirit.

He is the gate to life
Through which He bids us come.
With open arms we are welcomed
To come and feast at His table.

The resurrection and the life,
Death could not contain Him.
He conquered the grave over sin and hell.
Hallelujah, He lives in glory.

The Alpha and Omega,
The beginning and the end--
He is "I Am that I Am."
There is no God but Him.

Psalm of Our Savior's Gifts

You did not leave us alone,
But You sent Your Holy Spirit
To inhabit our lives with joy and peace,
And enable us to hear Your voice.

You did not leave us without instruction,
You gave us Your Holy Word.
Everything we need can be found
In the truth of Your precious teachings.

You did not leave us without weapons.
In a world ripe for Satan's attacks.
You gave us Your holy armor
To clothe us in righteousness.

You did not leave us without hope.
Eternal life is given through the Son--
A life of peace, beauty, and joy
Despite all the darkness around us.

You did not leave us without love.
The purest love comes from You.
A love that nothing can take from us,
The unconditional love of the Father.

You did not leave us without blessings.
We can see them every day.
You give us all the things we need
To sustain us and make us happy.

You did not leave us without beauty.
The majesty of Your creation is all around.
Not the beauty the world can give,
But the beauty of Your presence.

You did not leave us without protection.
Your angels guard us every day.
You put Your hedge around us
And cover us under Your wings.

You did not leave us without forgiveness.
All we must do is repent.
The blood of Jesus covers us all.
Our sin is forgiven in Him.

You did not leave us with fear.
There is no fear in Your love.
We can have peace in every storm
Because we know You are there.

You did not leave us forever.
Soon we will see Your return.
Every eye will see, and every knee shall bow,[7]
When You descend from the heavens.

We praise Your holy name
You did not leave us or forsake us.
Though sin is all around us,
We can rest in Your mercy and grace.

Psalm to the God of All

Awesome, almighty ruler of the universe,
Breathtaking and beautiful is Your countenance.
Creator of all heaven and earth,
Divine wisdom is in Your hand.

Eternal Father, who cannot fail,
Faithful are You to Your children.
Glorious is Your reign on high,
Hallowed be thy name.

Infinite love flows through You,
Jehovah God, my Lord.
King of kings and Lord of lords--
Messiah who came to save.

Nature rejoices and praises You,
Omniscient, Omnipotent King.
Powerful are You in might and strength,
Quintessential God of all.

Redeemer of the sins of the world,
Staggering is Your love.
Thunder and lightning are at Your command.
Undeniable power is Yours.

Veritable ruler of life are You.
Wonderful is Your Name.
Exalted on Your heavenly throne--
Yahweh, great God of all.

Psalm to the Bigness of God

As I contemplate Your greatness,
In awe I struggle to define You.
In my limited capacity,
I stand in total wonder of You.

You are the Creator of all that is
You spoke all of it into being
As far as the eye can see and further
With only a wave of Your Hand.

You created the massive universe,
Larger than our finite minds can comprehend.
Hundreds of billions of galaxies
Hung in space by Your Hand.

Millions of billions of stars you placed.
You number each one and call it by name.[8]
The skies proclaim the works of Your Hand[9]
The heavens proclaim Your glory.

How big You must be, how mighty and strong,
To create the expanse of space.
Just that one part of all You made
Is beyond human comprehension.

As if that were not enough,
You created the earth and the majesty in it.
A world full of wonders, both large and small,
You placed in exact precision.

Lastly, You created man
Different from anything else.
You gave him a soul and a consciousness;
Then breathed Your own breath into him.

Someone with whom You could communicate--
Someone to care for Your creation.
Someone who could be aware
Of Your majesty and Your power.

Man, who You said was Your best creation,
Is so small in comparison to the universe.
Yet, You gave him the ability to know You
And the gift of understanding.

How could a God who is big enough
To create worlds and all their workings
Be loving enough to come down to earth
To knit man together with His hand?

How big is Your heart, that set planets spinning?
Yet, You came down to love mankind.
You are omnipresent among all things.
You dwell in our hearts and our minds.

You cannot be measured by any tool of man.
You are infinite in Your presence.
You are transcendent beyond anything we know.
You were there before all creation.

You exist beyond all time and space.
Nothing can contain You.
You created the universe with just one thought.
So what is man that of him You are mindful?

Your great love reaches down to dwell with man.
You seek us out to be with You.
You know our thoughts, number the hairs on our head,
And You give us all our days.

My feeble mind cannot fathom Your ways
Or the mere existence of all Your creation.
Your holiness is beyond all comprehension,
And your glory to resplendent to behold.

How big You are, O Holy God--
Bigger than anything we can describe;
Bigger and wider than the universe.
Yet, You are in the tiniest detail.

O Holy God, I bow my knees
In worship and awe of You.
One day I will see Your face,
And I will know You just as You are.

Psalm of God's Faithfulness

Praise the Lord, O my soul,
And forget not all His benefits.[10]
Sing a song of His mighty acts
To His people through all of creation.

From the beginning of time,
He has guided His people.
Victory after victory He has given
And rewarded their faithfulness.

He has forgiven our sins time after time.
He has called us back to His side.
Without anger or malice, He sends His love
To redeem His people again.

His faithfulness has never waned.
He sees and provides for His own.
He hears every call, every prayer, every cry;
His love never leaves us alone.

He gives strength in our weakness
And comfort in sorrows.
He makes our paths straight
And guides us with His light.

A shield and refuge, He always remains
In times of trouble and strife.
He provides a way for His people
To escape from evil temptation.

His glory radiates from east to west
Never changing but always the same.
His love He gives unconditionally,
Even when it is not deserved.

O Lord most high, how faithful You are.
You are so wonderful and awesome.
Your countenance shines with glory and love.
We praise You forever and ever.

Psalm of Our Messiah

Prophets of old had foretold
Of a King who would save His people.
For hundreds of years people yearned to see
The Savior who would set them free.

People expected a King with a crown,
Riding on a regal steed.
People expected an army led by the King
To rescue them from oppression and need.

No one expected a baby;
Certainly not in a manger.
No one expected a lowly maiden
To give birth to the King of Kings.

Angels revealed the coming
Of the tiny babe so meek.
But the people could not understand
How this baby could be God's plan.

For 30 years the child grew in wisdom.
All were astonished in His presence.
Although just a child, He already knew
The purpose for which God had sent Him.

His ministry began, almost unknown,
But soon everyone knew His name.
He selected 12 to be His closet friends
To teach them what was to come.

People gathered in throngs to see Him.
They were amazed at His kindness and wisdom.
Everywhere He traveled throughout the land.
The masses grew bigger and bigger.

He healed and restored many people
They reached out to the miracle worker.
No one had ever known such a man,
Who spoke with so much compassion.

Many accepted Him as God's own Son,
The Redeemer of their nation.
But there were those who turned away
In fear they would lose their power.

They did not know who He really was.
Their eyes were blinded by sin.
They would not accept that such a humble man
Could be their Redeemer and King.

They scorned Him and mocked Him; they called Him a fraud.
They sought to discredit His words.
They refused to believe His teachings of love.
He was turned away by His own people,

Then came the day that all the earth dreaded.
Even creation knew who He was.
God's plan was revealed in the life of His Son,
His plan to save the world.

Jesus Christ, His only Son,
A man of sorrows became.[11]
He was betrayed in sin by one of His own
For 30 pieces of silver.

It was in the Garden of Gethsemane
He fell on His face before His Father--
To plead for His own life but willing to give it.
He knew what must be done.

He was taken by soldiers and delivered for trial
Even though He was totally innocent.
He was beaten and mocked and spit upon.
Yet, He said not a word in defense.

Then the people, who were called God's own
Cried out for his death in hate.
The very ones He had come to save
Spat anger and spite in His face.

Through beatings and mocking, He said not a word.
Yet, His suffering on earth would not end.
The cruelest of fates still awaited our Lord
As a cruel cross was placed on His back.

Up a hill called Golgotha, the Place of the Skull,
He struggled to stay on His feet.
The weight of the world was on that cross.
A heavier burden has never been carried.

They nailed His hands and feet to that cross.
Every blow of the hammer was so cruel.
The crown of thorns they had placed on His head
Pierced tissue and bone with each blow.

As they lifted Him up for all to see,
His arms outstretched in agony.
Every sin of the world came crashing down
Upon Him for you and for me.

He hung there before those who had condemned Him
As laughter and mockery they hurled.
Yet with a voice full of pain and love He cried,
Father forgive them, they do not know what they do.[12]

The skies turned black and the lightning flashed.
The whole earth began to tremble.
His blood poured out from His body and soul
As He gave up His life to save ours.

God the Father had to turn away.
He could not look at His Son.
The darkness and sin of the world on His own
He could not look upon.

Alone in the darkness, consumed with agony,
Jesus cried to His Father, "It is done."
Then He hung his head and let His life slip away,
But His purpose and mission were not yet done.

He was taken from the cross and buried in a tomb
By the ones who had called Him Master.
Distraught with confusion, they could not believe,
That their Savior was dead and gone.

He had told them the truth of His mission--
How His life was required in submission.
But they had not understood when He told them "rejoice,"
For after three days He would rise from the dead.

On the third day women came to anoint Him.[13]
They brought spices and oils for His body.
But the tomb, they saw, was open and empty.
The body was gone, He had risen!

Praise the Lord on High, He is not there.
Death can no longer enslave us.
We have been set free for all eternity
By the sacrifice of Jesus.

He loved so completely that He gave His own life
To save us from sin and death.
We now are God's children through the blood of His Son.
He has given us life everlasting.

Psalm of the Works of the Holy Spirit

The Holy Spirit is a mystery.
It cannot be seen or touched.
It is the supernatural dwelling
Of God's presence in the soul.

God the triune being
Knew we would need His presence.
He sent His Spirit to be with us
To comfort us in every trial.

When a person accepts Christ as Savior,
The Holy Spirit is given as a gift.
It is the infinite, eternal presence,
Of God's power within His children.

The Holy Spirit is God's hand
Placed within our soul:
God's own Holy presence,
Unchanging in loyalty and love.

The Holy Spirit in a child of God
Is the voice of God in our being.
It speaks to us wisdom and understanding
When we seek to know His will.

The Holy Spirit is goodness and truth,
God's holiness and His grace
That takes up residence within
To make us more like Christ.

The Spirit is God's agent
To bring messages to our soul.
It shows us meaning for our life
That gives us purpose and fulfillment.

The Spirit shows us God's grace
So that we can live more like Him.
We can have grace for others
When God's Spirit dwells within.

The Holy Spirit gives us comfort
When we feel sorrow or regret.
It gives us courage to keep going
In the face of the deepest pain.

The Spirit gives us knowledge
As we study the Word of God
It helps each one to find what they seek
In the mysteries of the Scriptures.

The Holy Spirit is the warmth we feel
As we pray and praise the Lord.
Its presence gives us peace
When the world seems so cold.

The Spirit prompts us to move
In the direction God has for us.
It is the Hand of God leading
To His paths of righteousness.

The Spirit is our intermediary
To God and all His power.
The Spirit prays and groans for us
When we are too lost to speak.

God's love dwells within us
By the presence of His Spirit.
We can know the true meaning of love
As it works within us to help others.

God's Spirit gives us courage
To fight against evil and wrong.
It assures us God is with us
Protecting us by His might.

Thank you, God, for sending
Your Spirit to live in Your children.
It is our blessed assurance
That You are present within us.

Psalm to the Blood of Jesus

O the precious blood of Jesus,
Blood He spilled out for me.
If not for that blood shed willingly,
No hope in this life could I see.

The blood He shed is not just a symbol.
It is still active and working today.
It covers His children from head to toe
Giving them life beyond this existence.

Jesus blood makes us righteous.
Under it we can enter the presence of God.
Without that blood we could never hope
To be good enough to seek Him.

That sacred blood sanctifies us.
It makes us holy in His eyes.
He forgives our sins and gives us hope
From the evils that seek to destroy us.

Peace comes from that flow of blood.
We can forever rest in His promises.
I know without a doubt I am held in His hands.
Nothing of earth can destroy me.

He is there with His children wherever they are
In calamity, uncertainty, and doubt.
He will never ever leave them alone
When they are covered with His blood.

Jesus's blood is full of healing
For a sound body, mind, and soul.
No matter what may affect us on earth,
It will be destroyed in heaven.

The spilled blood of Jesus is a promise
For our provision every day.
He will give us everything we need
Filtered through His loving Hand.

Our Shepherd He will always be.
He will seek us if we stray from His fold.
His eyes are always on His children.
He covers them with the fragrant oil of love.

God is our banner, our fortress, and shelter.
We are free from the fear of death and hell.
His blood won the battle with evil on earth.
He is the Lord of all.

O, how beautiful is the blood of Jesus.
It is a treasure beyond all measure.
At the end of time, nothing will matter
If we are covered by His blood.

Thank you, Lord, for the sacrifice
You so willingly gave for all.
Adoration and praise we lift to You
For the blood that covers and frees us.

Psalm to the Almighty

Awesome God, You are beyond all imagination.
Nothing can come close to comparing with You.
Almighty Father, who created all the earth,
Your power is unfathomable.

Beautiful is Your essence.
Your glory shines over Your children.
Benevolent is Your judgment,
Showing mercy to all who repent.

Comforter of Your people,
You never leave them alone.
With care You watch over everyone,
Enveloping them in Your hand.

Deliverer of mankind
From the clutches of Satan's grasp--
The Divine personage You are,
Who leads Your people to safety.

Everlasting Father,
Giver of eternal life--
You equip Your children
To prosper in times of trouble.

Faithful Father, from generation to generation,
You never withdraw from Your people.
Fearless are You in Your pursuit of them
To bring them to Your side.

Great and Glorious Lord,
Greatly are You to be praised.
Your glory shines brighter than the sun,
So bright we cannot look upon it.

Holy, Holy, Holy,
Lord of might in battle--
Hands are lifted to You in praise,
Hymns of worship are sung to Your name.

"I Am," the God of all things,[14]
Past, present, and future.
Infinite is Your love and Your mercy
Throughout all time and space.

Jehovah, Lord of the heavens,
Justice lies in Your hand.
Holy judge of all You are.
The last judgment will lie with You.

King of Kings, You came as a baby,
Born in a stable so meek.
You brought salvation to all mankind
By giving Yourself away.

Loving, living God,
Lord of Lords are You.
Nothing can usurp Your power
Nor come near to Your might and strength.

Marvelous is Your name.
Magnificent is Your honor.
Mighty is Your strength,
Magnanimous are Your blessings.

New every morning is Your faithfulness.
You provide daily for Your children.
As we wake to Your presence among us,
We feel Your Spirit working within.

Omnipotent are You in Your power.
Omniscient Your eyes see all.
Omnipresent are You in each life.
We cannot hide nor flee from You.

Precious Father, You are my treasure.
Your worth cannot be counted.
Your promises do not fail.
Your plan for each one is perfect.

Righteous Redeemer of all,
You gave Your own life for mankind.
You suffered and bled and died
That, through You, I am worthy of mercy.

Savior of the world,
Sorrowing servant You became.
Saving the lives of all people,
Sanctifying each one in Your name.

Three in One, Holy Deity,
You are true to Your Holy Word.
Father, Son, and Holy Spirit,
Alive and working within us.

Unchangeable, Unshakable, God only wise,
Your knowledge is unfathomable.
Unparalleled power is Your hand.
There is nothing equal to You.

You are the victor of the grave,
Working vengeance on the evil one.
You are the vine on which we grow
To become Your emissaries on the earth.

Worthy are You of praise,
Worthy of honor and glory--
Worthy of all the worship we can give,
Worthy of majesty and exultation.

Joyfully I will praise You
With everything that is in me.
I will sing of Your majesty and glory.
I will bow in worship to You.

Yahweh, God of the ages,
You existed before all of creation.
You knew us before we were formed,
And You appointed all our days.

Zealous are You in Your pursuit
Of those who will surrender their lives.
You bid everyone to come to You,
To live with You forever.

SECTION 3

PSALMS OF CREATION

Psalm of the Earth

How beautiful and wondrous,
Is Your creation, O God.
All that we behold
Shows the majesty of Your creation.

Magnificent and mighty are the mountains,
Raising their snow-capped tips to the sky.
Their strength and beauty, their hills and valleys,
Reflect Your might and Your power.

The roaring seas, teeming with life,
So vast they seem never ending.
The power of the water and waves
Displays Your image in their brilliance.

Deserts so vast and arid
Have powerful dynamics in the sand.
Many millions of grains, as vast as the stars,
Each one moving and shaping the land

Mysterious and ferocious jungles,
Holding animal and human life.
Rain forests, created to support all life,
You made to stabilize the environment.

Frozen lands were created by You
To maintain the earth's water supply.
Gigantic glaciers float in the seas,
A testimony to the immensity of You.

Rivers run their courses across the world,
Supplying vital and life-giving water.
Mighty waterfalls give life and power
To the smallest and largest of Your creatures.

Plains full of life-giving grain,
You created so that we would not hunger.
Our lives are enriched by the nutrients they give,
Supplying strength and growth for our bodies.

From the tallest, strongest mountain,
To the tiniest of seeds
Everything that You created,
Is intended for our good.

All the earth reflects Your wisdom,
Your strength, Your beauty, and Your provision.
Man is surrounded by a witness of You
If only we take the time to see it.

Psalm of Nature

In the early morning, the beauty of Your creation begins to emerge.
As I gaze out my window and see the majesty before me,
My breath catches in my throat in wonder
As the world unveils its beauty.

When I walk in Your creation,
The intricacy and components of the earth amaze me.
I know that only You could conceive of such beauty.
The things I see before me show Your power.

Who could make the tree standing in majesty
With each part doing its own job that makes it grand?
Who could know how to make the flowers thrive
In so many colors, shapes, sizes, and smells?

The grass in the meadows show different shades
As the sun and the shadow overcome it.
The wind blows it this way and that in its wake,
And its soft rustling speaks of Your glory.

I take off my shoes and walk in the green coolness.
I feel the softness and am reminded of Your presence.
I smell the fragrance as my feet crush the blades,
And I breathe in Your smell from the earth.

The sun glints off the rocks and the stones,
Their striations creating a map like Your heavens.
Oh, that I could follow them to Your heart
And sing praises unto You with their strength.

From the ground comes provision for my body and mind.
The bounty of Your creation feeds my life.
How thankful I am that You know what I need,
And You give it all freely from Your heart.

I raise my eyes to the mountains
And let the colors and shapes wash over me.
I hear the gurgling brooks and rushing water cascading down the hills.
I see the pureness of Your water sparkling in the sun.

I pick up a stone worn smooth by the rushing waters,
And I am reminded of the power in Your hand.
The power of regeneration and cycles of life
Give me hope for the future of the world.

I look to the sea with its great depth and width.
The power in the great waves that wash to and from the shore.
All its creatures, both great and small,
Were created by Your mind and Your hand.

The tiny cells so small my eyes cannot behold
The great and powerful creatures of the deep.
The mysteries in the waters, my mind cannot comprehend,
Show how small is my understanding.

The sun, the light, the moon, the stars,
The day, the night, the cycles of the earth
Perceived from Your mind to provide a way
To know the passage of time.

I marvel, O God, at the works of Your hand.
Nothing was left to chance.
From the tiniest atom to the brightest star
Everything set in its place.

How great, how mighty, how amazing are You Lord.
All the mysteries of life You created.
They are too numerous for me to imagine.
Your creation shows Your wisdom.

You gave all to me for my pleasure and my good.
The workings of nature bind together for my purpose.
You knew before creation just what I would need,
And You reached out Your hand for me.

Psalm of Reflections on a Day at the Beach

I stand on the beach looking out at the ocean
In all its vastness and power.
I watch the waves as they form,
Then break and spread over the shore.

The pull of the tide when I enter the water,
Is insistent in its power.
It has such potential to carry me away
As it recedes back into the ocean.

Shells are deposited on the beach--
Once homes to creatures tiny and large.
The ocean proves the destruction water can do
As it swirls and moves underneath.

The power of the ocean is so like the world
With its push and pull to take me away.
The waves are like temptations,
Never ceasing and strong on my life.

Beautiful to see and hear,
Temptation could easily sweep me under its spell.
But the destruction that occurs underneath
Has the potential to drown and destroy.

The sun beats down on the water and waves
And all those who come to enjoy it.
It will burn and scorch everything in its rays,
Leaving pain and misery behind.

Those who know its burning power
Seek measures to protect themselves.
Instead of pain in the aftermath,
They are able to enjoy it.

So, it must be as God burns away the dross
Of a life surrendered to sin.
The refining process of cleaning the soul
Is so painful unless we prepare.

I feel the wind, generated by the sea.
It cools and refreshes in the heat.
It blows and shifts everything in its path,
Changing the landscape and moving the sand.

Nothing is the same after the wind passes by.
The sand is displaced in its wake.
Everything that moves with the wind
Becomes new or is destroyed.

It is the same with God's saving breath.
It blows our sins completely away.
We are made new as it passes by.
Our lives are reshaped in its wake.

Footsteps in the sand,
Going back and forth along the beach.
They remain until the waves roll in
And wash them away to oblivion.

Much the same as we live our lives,
We leave footprints wherever we go.
We hope to leave a way to follow
To those who come after.

Death too soon arrives,
Washing our footprints away.
For each must make his own way
According to his own choices.

Each of us must seek the way
That God has prepared for us.
Each one is unique in his journey,
Not following a path already tread.

In everything and everywhere,
We can see the hand of God.
All that He created displays
His power and His wisdom.

Psalm of Two Adams

In all of creation nothing is so grand
As the man God made in His image.
A man created to commune with God,
To be blessed with God's own presence.

God named the man Adam because he was the first.
He was the beginning of all mankind.
He was placed in a garden of beauty and delights
And given dominion over the earth.

He was given a helpmate created from his own rib
To be his partner and lifelong wife.
"Populate the world" they were told by God
In unity and perfection.

There was only one rule they must obey
Without question or reasoning.
Do not eat of the tree that was placed by God
In the center of everything.

Even then, in all of God's perfection and peace,
Satan was plotting man's downfall
By tempting the woman to eat from God's tree,
Then share its fruit with her husband.

Only one rule was to be obeyed.
Yet, Satan's temptation was strong.
The downfall of man came crashing to earth
When Adam and Eve let him in.

God's glory was removed from man that day.
From perfection they were cast out.
The sin of one couple doomed perfect peace
To lives of struggle and pain.

Separated from the presence of God,
Death and punishment became man's reality.
No matter how much they tried to do right,
It was impossible to live up to perfection.

For thousands of years man sought to please God,
But they could not be righteous on their own.
The evil of man's heart always came back
To turn them in the wrong direction.

Yet, God in all His mercy and wisdom,
Longed to bring mankind back to Himself.
He had so much love for the ones He'd created,
He made a way to redeem them.

God knew all along we could not save ourselves,
No matter how many laws we obeyed.
He made a way in His goodness and mercy
To bring back His children to Him.

Jesus Christ, the Son of God,
Was sent to earth to save us.
He came as a human to relate to mankind,
To learn the human equation.

Jesus, too, was tempted by evil.
Satan offered Him the world.
Like the first Adam so long ago,
Jesus had to make a choice.

Into the darkness of the world He came.
It was the fruit of the fall in the garden.
He came to restore God's glory to man
As it had been in the beginning.

Christ experienced the same things we do every day.
He was tempted and pursued by Satan.
He was persecuted by His own people
And betrayed by those He trusted.

He went about teaching and preaching
To show people the way to God.
Many believed as they saw His miracles,
But others were controlled by Satan.

While being sought out by evil,
He went to a garden to pray.
Just like the first Adam, He had to decide
To succumb to the flesh or obey.

He chose to obey His Father;
Gave Himself up to be disgraced.
He did not betray His purpose
Even though it meant His death.

He was beaten and abused.
Yet, He said not a word in defense.
He was condemned to die on a cruel cross
By the people who feared His power.

Giving up His life and shedding His blood
On a hill called Golgotha,
Jesus became the Savior of all,
Restoring to man God's glory.

But death could not hold Him in the darkness of the grave.
God breathed new life into Him.
Defeating Satan and all evil on earth,
God's Son gave us a new beginning.

He ascended to His Father.
He told us not to be afraid.
He would prepare a place for us
To reign with Him forever.

Thanksgiving and praise to our Savior and Lord
For the second Adam who gives eternal life.
He restored man's communion with the Father above
That once again we may walk with Him.

Psalm of My True Destiny

Who is the Lord of my life?
My Father who is in heaven.
Who is the Master of my soul?
The Lord God great and mighty.

God formed and fashioned this body
In all its intricacies and wonders.
He breathed life into my lungs.
He placed strength within my bones.

The Lord of my heart is He.
No other could form such a marvel.
My heart beats the life blood within me
As it flows in intricate patterns.

He is the lover of my soul,
The place of my individuality.
He gives me free will every day
To choose my own destiny.

He is the Creator of my brain.
It is still such a wonder and mystery.
Even with all man's knowledge and skill,
The brain is still an amazing puzzle.

All the wonders of my body
Work together in perfect precision.
The exactness of each function
God determined before I was born.

Preciseness of the tiniest cell,
The meticulous workings within,
Are not a chance occurrence.
They were planned before time began.

God creates each child in His image.
There is nothing in creation that is random.
A gift from God are my body and soul,
Created as temples for His Spirit.

This body is only temporary.
It cannot exist indefinitely.
Each year I live in this flesh
Brings me closer to its end.

From dust I was created
And to dust this vessel will return.
But God's Spirit, who lives within me,
Will not die but will take me home.

I will be given a new body,
One that will live forever:
A body that is wondrous and perfect,
Not subject to earth's wear and decay.

I will live as God intended for me
In perfect peace and surrounded by beauty.
I will praise the Lord of creation,
Forever and ever and ever.

Death does not bring my end
In a grave where flesh decays.
It is only a path to my final home
And my true destiny.

Psalm of Shells

Hundreds of shells brought in by the waves
In all colors, shapes and sizes--
From tiny to large, they all have in common
The life that they once held.

Some are broken and filled with holes,
Worn and tossed by the ocean.
Others are ripped in so many pieces
They will never be whole again.

Many are beautiful and stand out in the sand.
Others are twisted and deformed.
Some shine in the sun like the stars of the night.
Others bury themselves in the sand.

It is as if they do not want to be seen.
They are ashamed of the way they look.
They cannot be displayed like the beautiful ones
Because they have been so broken.

There are those that are sharp and can injure or cut.
Others are worn smooth by the waves.
The sharp ones are avoided and left alone
While the smooth are picked up and cherished.

Small groups of shells cling together.
They are too frail to exist on their own.
Some attach themselves to ones larger than they.
They cling to the life of another.

Some look whole until they are turned over.
Then holes appear on the inside.
It is as if their hearts have been broken by stress
And part of them is missing.

Waves toss them on shore as if they are not wanted,
But some are reclaimed by the sea--
Only to be tossed and worn even more
Then spit out again and again.

There are those that become more beautiful
As they are tossed and turned in the tumult.
Yet, many are broken and shattered,
Not strong enough to withstand the furor.

So much like our lives are the shells on the beach.
We can look and see ourselves.
Life tosses and turns us in all different ways,
Not caring how much it hurts.

Some will stand strong and remain whole and stunning.
Others will be broken and destroyed.
It all depends on the foundations they have built
To withstand the tumult of life.

Not everyone is acceptable
In a world that values only beauty.
Some feel they must cling to the ways of the world
To have a successful life.

Doubt and guilt make some of us feel
We should bury ourselves in the sand.
Some feel so broken and hurt by the world
They want to hide away from others.

Just like those shells lying on the beach,
We are not all meant to be the same.
We are all different colors, sizes, and shapes.
That is the way we were created.

The difference between us and those shells
Is that we have a God who loves us.
He does not care what shape we are in,
Whether we are whole or broken.

We are His children, His finest creation.
He gave us life and His promise.
No matter what circumstance or condition we are in,
His love will never fail us.

Though we may be tossed and worn by the world,
We are never thrown out of His sight.
When life tears us and breaks us apart,
He is there to put us back together.

Thank God, we will never end up like those shells,
Tossed on the shore and abandoned.
We will never be left for the elements to destroy.
He will always be there to heal us.

SECTION 4

PSALMS FOR CHILDREN AND FAMILIES

Psalm of Love

Love is what we are born to seek.
Our hearts are not fulfilled without it.
We spend our lives here looking for love,
But it is ever elusive and frail.

The love that this world gives
Will never satisfy completely.
There are always expectations and hopes
That it simply cannot fulfill.

The love of a husband and wife
Makes the couple complete.
The love of a parent to child
Is a force greater than any other.

Love brings a family together.
It is the glue that holds it fast.
Love shared with others around us
Gives us joy and happiness in life.

But is this earthly love true?
Is it strong and everlasting?
Too often it disappoints and leaves us in despair.
We expect it to be perfect with never any care.

Other kinds of earthly love bring us to destruction:
Love of money, love of things, love of self.
Love of evil, love of pleasure, love of control,
Become hateful and arrogant in the end.

The world says that true love is only a myth;
That no one can meet its requirements.
We fall in and out of love in a moment,
But this kind of love never lasts.

What is this perfect love our hearts seek?
Where do we find this treasure?
It is there right in front of us always,
The unconditional perfect love of God.

God's Word gives us the secret
To having this love evermore.
It tells us the way of true and perfect love.
It shows the way to true happiness.

Love suffers long and is kind.[15]
It does not argue or accuse.
Love bears and believes all things.
It gives hope when we think there is none.

Love endures all things.
It does not give up on itself.
Even when it is betrayed,
Love gives another chance.

It does not judge or condemn
No matter how angry or hurt.
It does no harm to others
Even when it seems just.

Love does not seek hurt or revenge.
It is full of forgiveness and grace.
Love does not rejoice when another falls
But rejoices in the truth.

This true and unconditional love
Never fails or lets us down.
It seeks the good for everyone
Without earthly expectations.

The love of God is for what our hearts yearn.
Any other loves leave us seeking.
It is the kind of love we can build our life on,
The only love that gives true joy and fulfillment.

Earthly love of family and friends
Shall surely pass away.
But the true love of God stands forever,
Even when everyone else goes away.

We can have this love freely and clearly.
All we must do is accept it and live it.
For if we do not practice this love,
We will not be able to receive it.

Praise God, His love is everlasting,
Nothing we do can remove it.
The love that He offered His only Son
Is the same love He gives to you.

Psalm for Children

Do you know how loved you are little one?
Do you know that you are a miracle--
A miracle that was knitted together[16]
By the hand of the great Creator?

In all the multitude of shining stars,
You are more special than the brightest one.
In God's eyes you shine brighter
Than the brightest moon or sun.

Do you know that God loved you
Even before you were formed?
He put you together in an incredibly special way
And gave you a purpose to find.

God's angels rejoiced the day you were born.
They were with you when your mother first held you.
Your birth was a miracle from heaven,
And they witnessed how beautiful you are.

It is true, you know, those angels still guard you.
There is nothing they do not see.
They are God's agents assigned just to you
To protect you wherever you go.

Your parents love you with all their hearts,
But God loves you even more.
He knows every part of you, inside and out;
He formed your very heart.

Fingers, toes, eyes, and ears--
Every part of you was given a purpose.
From the tiniest cell to the largest limb,
Perfectly placed by the Creator.

There is no one on earth exactly like you.
You are one of a kind.
Of the millions of people all around the earth,
God made you unique, so you would shine.

Many people will love you in your journey on earth,
Especially those in your family.
Your birth was a wonderful time of joy
For those who were waiting to meet you.

Your parents would give their own lives for you
Because they love you so much.
They will teach you many new and wonderful things--
How to live in this world you were given.

There are so many things you will do and learn.
God created this world for you to enjoy.
He put you exactly right where you belong
To learn of His love for you.

First, you will walk, and then you will run.
You will laugh, and coo, and then talk.
You will grow a little every day of your childhood,
And too soon you will be an adult.

No matter how fast you may run,
No matter how far you may roam;
You can never outrun the love of your God
Nor go far from His reach as you are His own.

How precious you are in His sight, little one.
How He loves you with all His heart.
He made you to love and be loved from the start.
From the depths of His soul you came, and you are.

Psalm to Parents

God, You created mankind
To live in the likeness of You.
You gave us a heart to search for You,
And to understand who You are.

You gave us the desire to create new life,
To carry on Your legacy.
We want to bring progeny into our lives
So that our family name will be continued.

A baby, what a precious blessing
Given by God for us to cherish.
Our responsibility to You and this child
Is the most important thing we will ever have.

This child, placed by You in the womb
Was knit together by Your own hand.
You knew this child before it was formed.
You already set in motion Your plan.

Fearfully and wonderfully formed by You,[17]
You made this child's innermost being.
You set it apart to be Your child;
To bring it into Your Kingdom.

Given a special place in our hearts,
We are charged with the care of this child--
To bring it up in the way of the Lord,
To set an example of the way to live.

We are to love and provide for this child.
We make sure all its needs are met.
To provide a happy God-filled home,
To teach the child right from wrong.

Children are special to the Lord.
They are a part of His heart.
He gives them to us as a heritage,
Generation after generation.

God so loves all the children,
He assigned His angels to watch over them.
He warns us never to despise or reject them[18]
For His angels are keeping their guard.

Children are a treasure to value and adore
To encourage and nourish in the way of the Lord.
We are to love them with all reverence and awe
And see them as a gift from on high.

We are to give them a foundation
That will prepare them to go out in the world.
To teach them how to stand strong
When temptation and trouble beset them.

Above all, they must learn about love,
The unconditional love of God:
Love that keeps no record of wrong,
Love that forgives without thought.

Help them to see how much they are loved,
By you, and the God who made them.
Teach them to respect all children of God
And to know that God loves them all.

This tiny baby we hold in our arms
Will too soon grow out of our homes.
We must show them and teach them with all our love
To honor and revere their God.

Thank you, Lord, for this great honor.
You have put Your trust in us
That we might bring up these tiny beings
To be who You made them to be.

May our prayers and our love for these children
Follow them for as long as they live.
May their lives be filled with blessings
Because we have been faithful.

Psalm of My Legacy

My greatest hope and desire
Is to leave a legacy for my children and grandchildren--
Not of money or earthly possessions,
But of the things of God they see in me.

To leave a legacy of prayer
Is the greatest thing I could give them--
A knowledge that prayer is their weapon,
Their shield and fortress forever.

To seek God in everything they do.
To have discernment and wisdom.
That God's Word would be their guide
To live in a world gone wrong.

To have honor, respect and love for God,
To praise Him in all things.
That they put Him first in their hearts and lives
And never waver in their convictions.

To have grace and compassion for others,
To reach out in time of need.
Grace to love when all around is hatred,
Grace that forgives without question or judgement.

To have peace in all things good and bad,
The peace that only comes from Jesus.
The peace of their salvation
And everlasting life.

Father, let my children remember me
As a praying mother and grandmother.
Let my prayers for them not lie fallow
But sustain them for all their lives.

This legacy I leave to my descendants
To become the children of God--
To dedicate their lives to Him,
And be an example to the next generation.

Psalm of Heroes and Princesses

Most every little girl,
When she gets to a certain age,
Wants to be a princess;
To live a fantasy life.

Little boys all aspire
To be a superhero,
Doing crazy, impossible stunts;
Saving the world in the process.

Indoctrinated by movies
And modern media devices,
Even story books from long ago
Give visions of a fairy tale life.

Encouraged to play these imaginary roles
Give pleasure and sweet dreams.
Costumes and make believe
Inspire children's imaginations.

Too soon they all find out
All dreams do not come true.
Everything is not sweetness and light
In the world in which we live.

Princesses are not always rescued
By their sought-after handsome prince.
Superheroes cannot really fly.
Too often, evil wins.

How much easier the transition would be
If they were all taught from the beginning.
Fairy tales will not come true,
But there can always be a happy ending.

All little girls are truly princesses,
In the Kingdom of the Lord.
They are already born to royalty
As daughters of the Most High King.

Boys are princes in His sight.
They are even given superpowers.
The King gives them everything they need
To overcome every evil rival.

All those little girls and boys
With dreams bigger than the sky
Can truly see those dreams come true
In the Fathers plan for their lives.

There is not one child ever created,
Who is not a hero or princess.
No matter the circumstance or place,
Each one is beautiful in the Father's eyes.

When a child comes to know the Lord as their God,
When they surrender their heart to Him,
Nothing can ever take them away,
From being an heir to His glory.

They will always be crowned with love from on high.
Joy will reign in their heart forever.
They will be given the keys to the Kingdom,
Ruled over by their Father, the King.

So, dream big dreams all you boys and girls.
You really are princesses and heroes.
You are daughters and sons of the King of the world
No greater honor can ever be given.

Psalm of Prayer of the Caregiver

Father in heaven, look down on me
For I am so very tired.
My mission here on earth has changed.
I never imagined I would be here.

I have been given the role of caregiver.
To someone whom I love.
This is not what I imagined
My life would ever be.

Lord, I am at a loss for what to do.
I am not trained or ready for this.
How do I handle this illness
That requires my every minute?

I feel so alone on this journey.
No one understands what I feel.
Please give me wisdom and strength.
Hold me in Your arms of love.

Give me patience in my spirit
To answer the same question over and over.
Help me contain my frustration
When things seem out of control.

It hurts so to see my loved one
Not able to care for himself;
To watch his memory fading
As he loses himself in a fog.

Show me how to love him
When he does not know who I am;
When he fights against all reason,
Give me strength to do what is right.

When medical emergencies arise,
Give me peace in the crises.
When my anger begins to overtake me,
Send peace into my soul.

Give me physical strength and stamina
To do whatever is needed.
Protect my body from harm
When he is not aware what he is doing.

Guard my thoughts, my reactions, my mouth
When words of frustration want to come out.
Help me understand that my loved one
Can still be hurt by my words.

Lord, let me always remember,
That You work all things for good;
That you hold me in Your arms
When things seem out of control.

I do not know why this has happened.
My heart cries out for a reason.
It screams, "there must be a way
To justify this illness."

When doctors and health care professionals
Admit there is nothing more they can do,
Give me faith that Your hand still holds me.
Let me believe and rest in You.

Keep me strong in faith and belief
That You see my every need.
Let me know there is nothing You do not control
When pain is all I can see.

As I watch my loved one slip away
Whether in body, in mind, or in spirit,
Give me love and faith in my heart
To know he will be whole again.

Lord, hold me in Your hand.
Filter this situation through Your love.
Send Your Spirit to minister to me
When I just want to give up.

Let my loved one know in his heart
That You love and are waiting to heal him,
Never allow him to slip so far away
That he does not feel Your Spirit.

Keep me going, Lord, every day
To minister in any way that is needed.
Let me rest when he rests and be ready
To meet his every need.

I know in my heart that You have us
Both in the palm of Your hand.
Send Your Spirit to minister to us
As we surrender each day to Your plan.

Psalm of Prayer for My Grandchildren

I will rejoice very greatly in You Lord
For You have given me grandchildren.
You have blessed me with unspeakable joy.
You have completed my heart on this earth.

The joy of holding these children,
Made by Your hand in Your Image,
Overwhelms my spirit with thankfulness
For this honor You have given.

Let me never forget Your faithfulness
As I pray for their minds, bodies, and souls.
May I never give my responsibility for them
To someone else to hold.

O Lord, make their little hearts tender
To know You even as babes.
Let my words and my actions show them
How to have faith and trust Your name.

Every day, as I fall to my knees,
Let my prayers for them fill Your ears.
As I pray for them to know You,
Place the desire in their hearts for You.

They will live in a world full of danger.
Their safety I place in Your Hands.
Put Your hedge of protection around them
And guard them in all their ways.

As they grow, give them bodies of strength
And keep them from diseases and illness.
Protect them from those who would hurt them.
Keep them safe in Your Hand.

O Lord, give them wisdom and discernment
To learn the right from the wrong.
Let their minds dwell in goodness and kindness
To be gentle and helpful to all.

Bless them Lord with compassion
For others not as fortunate as they.
Give them a desire to help people,
To share with them all that they have.

Let their eyes be filled with wonder
As they grow and experience the world.
Give them the ability to see beauty
In all Your world around them.

Send Your angels to watch over them
When fear grips their hearts and their minds.
Give them courage and faith to know
You will never leave them alone.

Above all, Lord, lead their hearts to You
To experience Your salvation.
Give them a yearning each day of their lives
To embrace more and more of You.

This world offers so many temptations.
It would be easy for them to go wrong.
O Lord, clothe them with Your armor
To withstand the evil around them.

Fill their lives with joy and happiness.
Let their laughter ring out every day.
In their lives give them friends and influences,
Who show them the joy of faith.

Make them aware of Your blessings.
Let them never take You for granted.
Show them how much You love them.
Saturate them with Your Spirit.

Give them the desire, in everything they do,
To bring honor and glory to You.
To prepare themselves to serve You each day
By studying Your Word.

Prepare the path You have for them
As they grow and become independent.
Keep their feet firmly planted in You, Lord,
And their faith rooted in Your Word.

Make the way ready for their future, Lord.
Send them spouses who dwell in You.
Bless their lives with joy and fulfillment,
The joy only found in You.

Let them stand as lions against evil.
Be great women and men of courage,
Help them spread Your message
To all those they encounter.

One day I will not be with them.
My prayers and love will be gone.
Let them remember me in love.
As one who led them to You.

I praise You, God, for these children,
These precious expressions of You.
I will love them and keep them for all my days
In my mind, in my heart, in my prayers.

Psalm on the Death of a Spouse

Lord in heaven, how am I to go on?
My loved one has died and left me alone.
The brokenness and sorrow I feel
Is overwhelming my spirit and soul.

I was not prepared for this, Lord.
Death takes us unawares.
It left me with such hopelessness.
My life is empty and reeling.

The grief of knowing full well
I will not see his face again
Has left me stunned and confounded,
All alone and not knowing my way.

This pain I feel every moment
Seems as if it will never go away.
My heart is broken in pieces.
Will it ever be restored?

Resentment boils up because he left me
All alone and not knowing the future.
I feel guilty for my angry thoughts.
Help me to know this is normal.

What will I do without him?
How can I manage to live?
He was my spouse, my friend, and father to our children.
He will be missed by all of us.

Father, I need Your presence
To feel Your Spirit touching my heart.
I am so weak and overwhelmed.
You are my only hope.

I know he is in Your presence,
I know he is not suffering there.
The knowledge of this is a comfort.
Yet, I yearn for him more and more.

Help me rest in Your presence, Lord.
Set my heart and soul at ease.
Give me comfort and peace in knowing
This is not the end; I will see him again.

I place my future in Your hand, Lord.
I do not know what to expect now.
Calm my weary spirit with Your peace.
Cast anxiety away with Your Spirit.

I thank You that You are here, Lord,
That You have never left my side.
You see my tears of sorrow
And feel them as Your own.

I am so grateful for Your love:
A love greater than any I have known.
I could not go through this on my own
Without You holding my hand.

Father, I await the day
When I will see You in Your glory;
When I will see my spouse in Your heaven
Already singing Your praise.

Psalm of Letting Go

As I sit in this hospital room,
Watching my dad's life slip away,
My heart is filled with sorrow;
Tears roll down my face.

I hold his hands, so frail and weak.
How wrinkled and worn they look.
How strong and sure they were once in his life--
Those hands I thought could do anything.

This is not what he wanted
For his mind and body to betray him.
The man he was is gone.
He is in a place he does not belong.

My heart breaks and shatters
When he asks me who I am.
After 69 years of being my Dad,
He no longer knows my name.

As he lies there and asks, "Where am I now,"
I try to explain it with love.
His mind can no longer comprehend
The words I am saying to him.

Oh, how I wish I could tell him
He will soon be in a place of peace.
The Lord has not forgotten him.
His suffering will soon come to an end.

Sometimes I see a spark
Of the man he used to be.
Something he is remembering
From the past when he was free.

So many happy times with him
Come to my mind and heart--
Things that I will remember
For the remainder of my life.

There were bad times, too,
When he abandoned us.
Without explanation he withdrew from our lives,
Leaving us devastated.

Feelings of hurt and confusion
Took an awfully long time to heal.
But whatever his reasons and actions were,
I loved him enough to forgive.

No matter what has happened,
My daddy he will always be.
I am going to pray for him
And love him till the end.

I cannot help but wish death would come quickly
To release him from this affliction.
Let him close his eyes in death
To open them in heaven.

He lifts his hands to the ceiling,
His eyes see something I cannot.
I know the angels are calling to him,
"Son of the Father, it is time to come home."

I tell him it is ok to go,
Not to worry about the ones he is leaving.
We will look forward to joining him
In a single blink of God's eye.

We all want him to remain
But not as he is now.
Our sorrow will be great indeed,
But we will rejoice that he is in heaven.

There God will restore his mind.
He will be given a new body.
No longer will he suffer this pain and confusion
But will worship and praise His Lord.

Thank the Lord we have His assurance
That death is not the end.
It is only a steppingstone to true life
Where we will be united again.

SECTION 5

PSALMS OF GOD'S PRESENCE AND ENCOURAGEMENT

Psalm of Quietness

As I go into my closet, and I fall upon my knees,
I feel the quietness of Your Spirit come to me.
Your love descends into my heart, and Your peace fills up my soul;
And I know that You are here to speak with me.

As I call upon Your precious name and give You all my praise,
I feel the burdens of my life begin to lift.
The load that is so heavy, I give into your hand,
And I know that You have saved me by Your grace.

O Lord, that I could dwell forever in this quietness,
Listening to the still small voice that comes to me.
For in this quietness I move into Your presence
And feel the wondrous love You freely give to me.

In holy quietness, I feel your presence
In holy quietness, I hear Your voice.
In holy quietness, I know Your power.
And in this quietness my spirit can rejoice.

Psalm of Battle

The battle inside me is raging.
The pull of the enemy is strong.
It is so easy to be what the world expects of me--
To give in as temptation pulls me on.

The fight seems to be growing harder.
My eyes begin to dim with fatigue.
Despair on every hand brings me falling to my knees.
Then His words reach to the inner part of me.

Fear not, little lamb, I am with you.
Go forth in My strength into the war.
I will not forsake you, nor leave you alone.
Fear not, go in peace, you are my own.

"Fear not," gives me strength in the battle,
"Go forth," keeps me going in the dark.
I know when all of me is what He wants me to be,
The battle is over, and He has won.

So, I will fear not for I know that He is with me.
I will go forth with His strength into the war.
He will not forsake me nor leave me alone,
I will fear not, I will go in peace, I am His own.

Psalm of Security

Hallelujah, Praise the Lord!
I am a child of the King
With all the rights and benefits
Through the blood of Jesus Christ.

I have been saved, justified, and sanctified.
He has forgiven all my transgressions.
His promises are true and everlasting.
I can dwell in the shadow of the Almighty.

I do not have to be afraid of anything.
My Father promised to deliver me from evil.
He covers me with His almighty wings
And is a fortress where I can hide.

I am surrounded by His loving kindness.
He is my hope, my truth, and my strength.
Goodness and mercy shall follow me
All the days of my life.

Even when I am in despair,
He is my light in the darkness.
Peace and security are mine to claim.
He will never leave or forsake me.

God is my help in time of trouble.[19]
He is my defense from which I shall not be moved.
He upholds me and keeps me in His faithfulness,
Mercy and blessing He continually proves.

In beauty and grace He clothes me.
He preserves my life forever.
He hears every prayer I utter to Him.
He always answers for my good.

I am fearfully and wonderfully made by His hand.[20]
In His own image He formed me.
My joy, my gladness, my faith, and trust
Are all given to me by His Spirit.

Everything I will ever need He has already provided.
I can see His wondrous works in my life.
He is my friend, my Savior, and King.
I put all my hope in Him.

My salvation is secured in Him.
He has given me life everlasting.
He is preparing for me a dwelling place
Where I will live forever with Him.

Hallelujah, Praise the Lord!
I am a child of the King.
I will behold Him and fall on my knees
When the end of my days has come.

Psalm of Our Savior's Plea

I came that you might have life, but you reject me.
I came that you might see, but you are blind.
I came to give you water. Yet, you still cry out in thirst.
Why my child, Oh why?

My word I gave to you, but still you wander in the dark.
My love I gave for peace. Yet, you struggle in despair.
My life I gave to save you. Still, you grope in sin and pain.
Why my child, Oh why?

I created all of life that you might have the best there is.
Yet, you wallow in the mud of your own making.
I shed all my blood for your healing. Yet, you die.
Why my child, Oh why?

I walked the road you walk so you will not stumble. Yet, you fall.
I bore the cross to set you free, yet you are bound.
I died for all your sin, still you turn your face from Me.
Why my child, Oh why?

Oh My child, My precious child, reach out and touch Me.
Come to me, receive the life I have for you.
Call My name and be cleansed from sin for I love you.
Oh My child, I call to you, take all of Me.

Psalm of War

Lord God Almighty, praise be unto You.
For You have given us freedom from evil.
By Your strong and mighty power
You have defeated the Satan who plagues us.

How then do we live in the evil of this world
When all around us we see its temptation?
What is our defense against the fear in which we live
When godly people are being persecuted?

What is our defense against the powers which beset us?
How do we stand up and fight
When we are surrounded on every side,
By an evil we cannot see?

You are our armor, our defender, and protector.
You are the strongest high tower where we can run.
You are defeating the evil so oppressive,
And we are Your soldiers in the fight.

Your armor is not made by man,
But it is from Your Divine hand.
No evil can penetrate its Holy creation.
You made it so that we might stand.

Our fight is not one of flesh and blood.[21]
It is not man against man.
We fight against powers, against darkness and evil,
Trying to take us from God's hand.

You have given us Your truth
Against which none can stand.
Against arrows of deceit and evil
Your righteousness covers our hearts.

Peace reigns in our minds
As we study Your Word.
We can stand up and fight
When we know the battle plan.

Faith gives us strength to raise our shield
For protection against darts flung toward us.
The wicked one's fire, wrath, and hate
Will not penetrate through us.

The sword of the Spirit is our defense.
We swing it against the enemy.
The Spirit will not fail when the battle is fierce;
When we have practiced using it.

Watch for the evil upon you,
Surrounding your very life.
Pray with all power to Almighty God.
Pray without fear or ceasing.[22]

Call out for the great power we have been given.
Call out and be assured
That God hears and sees and knows us well.
He will not desert us in the fight.

We praise You, O God,
For Your protection and Your peace.
There is no evil we cannot defeat
With You as our captain and King.

Psalm of God's Word

Thy Word is a lamp unto my feet[23]
And a light unto my path.
It brings wisdom and hope to my daily walk.
It is the everlasting truth.

The God-breathed Word of the living Lord
Is given to us as a guide.
It abides with us for everlasting time.
It will never pass away.

The powerful Word of God is as real today
As it was when it was written.
It is unfailing reality and truth.
It is as flawless as purified gold.

Sharper than a two-edged sword,[24]
It warns us away from sin.
It warns of the dangers of evil
And guides us to paths of righteousness.

His Word is the food and milk we need
To grow and mature in Christ.
It teaches, corrects, and guides us,
In His everlasting grace.

Nothing can ever change His Word.
It is good. It is right. It is true.
It is the unfailing and pure word of life;
Our source of wisdom and truth.

Active and living every day,
It will never be outdated.
The power and might in its totality
Is inspiration for holy living.

Psalms and hymns being raised to God
Are never ending within its pages.
The prayers and petitions of the past
Are just as relevant for us today.

His Holy Word lives and abides forever
No matter the year or the age.
The testimony of Jesus Christ
Will never pass away.

Lord, let Your Word abide in me.
It is my source of rejoicing.
Let my mind and spirit dwell day and night
In the wisdom it exposes.

No other word, no other book,
Is as precious and living today.
The Word given by God so long ago
Will live on for eternity.

Psalm of God's Love

I have loved you with an everlasting love,[25]
Says the Lord of love and light.
Nothing will ever take you from My hand
No matter what trouble may come.

I have put my banner of love over you
To protect and shelter you in darkness.
The love I have for you will never be shaken.
The mightiest storm cannot move it.

I love the sparrow and provide its needs.
How much more then will I provide for you.
You are the highest of My creation.
I loved you before you were formed.

Many waters will never quench My love for you.[26]
There is no force strong enough to do so.
Nothing you can ever do or be
Will remove My love from you.

I loved you so much that I gave my own Son,
The one who suffered, bled, and died.
In agony, He gave you My ultimate love.
What more could I do for you?

I desire to lavish My love on you
So that you will always feel safe.
I will be faithful to give My love
To My children whom I have made.

My love reaches to the highest heavens.
It extends from the east to the west.
It will be with you wherever you are.
You can never outrun its effect.

My unfailing abundance of love
Will always be with you, my child.
This is My promise to you ever more.
Never doubt My great love for you.

Psalm of Man

What is man that You are mindful of him?[27]
He is Your greatest creation.
You gave him dominion over all things
And made him a little lower than the angels.[28]

What honor You bestowed on man
When You made him in Your image!
The greatest, most humbling distinction
Was to separate man to Yourself.

How glorious You are O God,
How excellent is Your name.
You gave us the ability to praise You;
To lift Your name to the heavens.

No other creature of Your making
Is blessed with the knowledge of You.
The desire to know our maker
Was placed in man's heart by Your hand.

We have the high reward of Your presence,
Even when we do not deserve it.
You meant for us from creation
To be led and guided to You.

How amazed am I at Your love,
Your greatness, and Your wisdom.
I worship You for Your mercies.
In adoration I bow in reverence.

How thankful I am for this life--
The life You placed within me.
I give my life wholly to You,
It was already Yours from the beginning.

SECTION 6

PSALMS FOR DOUBT AND BROKENESS

Psalm of A Broken Heart

My soul cries out to You, Father,
From a heart that is broken and shattered.
The betrayal and hurt that fills my mind
Is so loud I cannot get around it.

The ones who I love the most
Have turned away and left me alone,
Flinging words of anger and hate,
Like arrows aimed straight for my soul.

Words that were from Satan,
Words that came from lies,
Words that tore my heart apart,
Clang in my ears like a gong.

The betrayal of whom I love,
The ones I would give my life for,
Have torn my life into shreds
With their words and hate-filled looks.

And now I am alone,
Separated from those I love--
Those who gave my life meaning;
Those who gave me a purpose.

The greatest of Your gifts to me
Has been taken in anger and malice.
My love has been ignored,
And my cries proclaimed as crazy.

O God in heaven, I cry out to you.
Deliver me from this anguish.
Take these thoughts and nightmares from my mind
And free me from despair.

You alone are my God, and my Father.
You are my only solace.
You are the one who can take this pain
And wash it away from me.

You are my only hope
To carry on in this life.
You are my only help
For this crushed and fragile spirit.

I cannot bear up under it.
I cannot continue to be
Without You as my deliverer
From the cruelty that is hurled at me.

O God, hear my cries,
Take this pain away.
Give me peace to live my life,
Please show me the way.

All of this hurt I give to You.
All those words that ring in my ears.
Take away all loneliness and despair
That makes me cry out my fears.

Fill my heart and my mind, O Lord,
With thoughts of your love and mercy.
Place Your hand on my heart and heal it.
Let Your grace wash over my soul.

For You have promised Your presence
Amidst all my tears and pain.
Take this heart in Your hand and heal it.
Make my heart and my life brand new.

All praise to You the Almighty
That I can run to your shelter
To be covered and loved by Your presence;
To be kept safe in Your Holy Spirit.

A Psalm of Addiction

I see you now for what you are addiction.
I hear you calling, calling, calling my name.
You block out everything but you from my mind.
Nothing seems to be true, or am I going insane?

I look in the mirror, and I see your face,
I do not even recognize that it is me.
You have taken control of me, inside and out.
My visage is blurred with your greed.

How long must I endure your pain and your pull?
What has my life become?
You separate me from my family and friends.
You alienate me from a life worth living.

What once felt so good to my body and mind
Has become images of terror.
Will you control me for all my days,
Or will I give in to your call for my life?

Whether it is alcohol, drugs, chemicals, food,
Technology, work, money, or more,
Each of these things want to make me believe
They will fill up the holes in my soul.

No! Nothing you give can fill me now.
Nothing you offer is good.
You are a liar, a thief, and a killer.
Only my death will satisfy you.

But wait, there must be someone or something
That can give me a reason for living.
Once in my life I remember a time
When every day was a joy and a privilege.

There was a time when my mind was filled with truth,
A reason for being and living.
There was a time when I never had to stand alone.
I knew where my strength came from.

O Lord, my God, help me to remember.
Come to me and cleanse my soul.
Take this evil within me and cast it away.
Over my life take full control.

Freedom is what I am asking from You--
Freedom from the strivings within me.
Your Word speaks plainly to all who believe
That whom God sets free is free indeed!

Give me strength as I battle this foe for my life,
Show me the way so I can run to the truth.
Show me grace when I slip; pick me up when I fall.
Set my feet on the Rock that is higher than I.

Only You, Lord, can make me whole once again.
Only You can forgive all my sin.
Your love can rescue me from this life
And blot out the transgression within.

Show me Your mercy and give me a new start.
Pick me up from this filth. Draw me near to Your heart.
I surrender myself to Your merciful hand,
I give over my life to Your all-knowing plan.

Addiction, you have no more power over me!
My mighty God has come to set me free!
He is stronger than you are or ever can be!
There is nothing He will not do for me!

Psalm of Desolation

O Lord, my heart is heavy within me.
I have been brought low by the world.
Doubts of who I am beat through my head
In a relentless chorus of guilt.

The loneliness and desolation I feel
Cannot be filled by anything of this world.
Those who condemn me, shout long and hard of my sin,
Taking joy in their condemnation.

Those who have turned away from me,
Hide their faces in snide superiority.
They laugh in their self-righteousness,
As they show who they truly are.

Lord, deliver me from the persecution and loneliness.
Send you Holy Spirit to calm my soul.
Touch my heart with Your loving presence
And make me know who I am.

For You are my Father and I Your daughter.
Your forgiveness surpasses all things.
Your grace and Your mercy reached out to bring me home,
And you loved me into Your kingdom.

Lord on high, take my plea and hear it.
Look into my soul and see the pain.
For You are my healer and my comforter.
Lord, You are all I need.

Psalm for the Sick

Hospitals, clinics, asylums, institutions--
Places for people who are sick.
Whether sickness of body, of mind, or of heart,
These are places of refuge for the ill.

People are filled with the darkness of evil.
People are physically ill.
People are searching to be filled. Yet, are empty.
People seek help for their soul.

There are people whose hearts are broken;
People with twisted minds.
There are people full of hate and malice;
People who need comfort and peace.

There are those with physical illness;
Some with cancer consuming their body.
So many diseases we cannot control
Are ravaging all ages.

Where is Thy healing touch, Lord?
We do not see Your miracles now.
Is our faith too little and our belief too small
To claim healing for ourselves?

Have we lost our ability to see and
To know that Your Word is true?
When do we remember Your promise
That You have overcome the world?

Broken bones, broken hearts, broken lives,
Broken minds, broken wills, broken spirits--
We see them all around with no compassion.
Lord, forgive our hardness of heart.

Our illness and pain are not of Your making.
Your promises still stand true.
Your blessings of health You desire to pour out.
On those who call out to You.

Lord, make us aware of Your presence
To know with assurance that You are here.
Let us believe in your healing
When our body is ravaged and sore.

Your mercies pour out from heaven--
Mercies of healing and love.
Let our be minds open to Your healing, Lord.
Let us not depend on the world.

For You are the God of all health,
Mind, body, and soul.
You are the God who can make us whole
When we open our hearts to You.

Psalm of Darkness

How long, O Lord, how long
Must this heart be covered by darkness?
My soul cries out to You for light
As the darkness pursues me day and night.

My eyes are blinded by the things of the world,
Valued so highly by man.
Perception becomes warped as I look to the world
To give me peace within.

Darkness brings jealousy, envy, and hate.
Men war with each other without pause.
Blinded by expectation am I,
But I am broken with disappointment instead.

The world says success is all I need
To be a person of worth.
I am tempted to crush those who block my path
As I climb the ladder of wealth and esteem.

Yet, emptiness pervades my soul
As water evades those who thirst in the desert.
My heart within me is empty and alone.
My spirit is filled with grief.

The success of the world leaves me empty,
Hungering for love, joy, and peace.
All I see is darkness and despair.
My soul cries out for relief.

Open my eyes that I may see, Lord,
The beauty of Your way.
Give me light that beckons me to give way
To sight in Your narrow way.

Let me live in Your light, Oh God,
So that nothing is worth more than You.
Grant that I be overcome by joy, love, and peace
When I keep my eyes upon You.

The world gives me darkness, ambition, and strife;
Tells me I am nothing without it.
But You give me light in Your love and Your grace
And assure me that I am worthy of it.

How shall I live, then, in darkness or light?
How shall I spend my life here?
Am I pursuing the world or clinging to You?
Give me strength, Lord, Your light to reveal.

Free my eyes from darkness.
Show me the light for my way.
Renew my mind in You, Lord,
Day after day after day.

For You are the light of all life.
You are the brightness of hope.
Your Word shows the way to live here and now
In the light of Your wonderful love.

Psalm of Prayer for Pain

Do You hear my cry, O God?
Do You see my tear-stained face?
Can You see my broken heart?
Do You care at all for me?

The pain that I feel is overwhelming.
It has plunged me into depths of despair.
So many times, I have cried out to You.
Yet, I do not feel Your presence near.

I do not know how to pray anymore.
My prayers seem to vanish in thin air.
I cry out to You in my suffering,
But the pain grows stronger each day.

Lord, I am so alone.
No one understands my pain.
You promised You would be with me,
But all I feel is forsaken.

My prayers cry out for relief.
Yet, this sorrow grows stronger each day.
How can I continue to live
When my whole life is in such disarray?

I am abandoned by those who once loved me.
They do not know how to comfort my pain.
Oh, that Your Spirit would only come
To share Your healing and love.

I cry out to You for relief, Lord,
I just want to be out of this world.
The pain that racks my body and mind
Makes me long to be home with You.

My earthly mind cannot stand to think
This pain will always be.
To live every day in such distress
Leaves me longing for death and peace.

O Lord, if I could just hear You;
Could feel the touch of Your hand.
If only I could see You;
Know You are working on my behalf.

God, take this pain away from me.
Let me feel Your loving care.
Set my mind and heart at peace
That Your comfort is already here.

Show me the way to find You
That I may rest in Your embrace.
Spread Your loving light around me.
Let me feel the warmth of Your grace.

I cannot live without You.
My soul and body are too crushed.
Lift me up in Your compassion.
Heal me with Your loving touch.

Show me how to see through this pain
To Your love, compassion, and healing.
Give me strength as I continue to live
To seek Your presence in every condition.

Psalm of Life's Disappointments

In this life we will experience
Disappointment on many levels.
It could be family or friends,
Even society around us.

The expectations we have been taught
For our rules and our behavior
Are sometimes more unrealistic
Than our earthly lives can achieve.

We become disappointed in our parents
When we discover they are not perfect.
We begin to realize as children
Even love cannot meet all expectations.

We are disappointed in a spouse,
Who does not live up to our ideal.
We expect them to make us happy;
To love us the way we are.

We look forward to a marriage,
Filled with happiness and love.
We believe this person we have chosen
Will be perfect in every way.

It is such a disappointment
When things start to go awry.
We argue, we fight, we condemn
When disappointment begins to creep in.

When our children begin to arrive
To make our family complete,
Joy and elation accompany them.
Surely, these children will be perfect.

One day they begin to talk back;
Rebellion enters their heart.
They disobey the rules we have
In an effort to be themselves.

These beautiful, perfect children,
We have poured our lives into
Break our hearts and worry our minds.
We shed tears of grief and disappointment.

Friendships are so precious.
We believe they will always last.
One day we discover our friend
Has used us for his own gain.

We all have expectations
Of the people who surround us.
Yet, people disappoint us
Every single day.

Even things that we look forward to
Can bring disappointment as well.
We desire all things to be how we dream them
When, in reality, they are not.

We disappoint ourselves
By not living up to our own expectations.
Our lives are not what we wanted to be.
We struggle with our own inadequacies.

Mankind is not perfect.
We live in a world of sin.
Selfishness, greed, and anger,
Cause us to hurt family and friends.

So, what is the point of a life
That cannot meet our expectations?
Why should we try to live rightly
When so many things go wrong?

Why should we try our best
To be a person of integrity
When all around us, in so many things,
All we see is disappointing?

Is there anything or anyone
That will not cause us disappointment?
Is there anyone or anything
That can be all that we expect?

We have a heavenly Father,
Who will never disappoint.
He offers us a life of perfection
Filled with joy and happiness.

His presence is a place of perfect peace
Where nothing will ever go wrong--
A place where all expectations
Will be met and more besides.

There is a place where we will be happy
And a place where we can rest.
He prepares a place for us
That will never disappoint.

His love for us is infallible.
He will never let us down.
He will never stray from the truth
Of the word He has always vowed.

He protects us and keeps us safe
From the evil that seeks to destroy us.
His peace will reign in our hearts,
Giving us joy and assurance.

We will not be disappointed
When we gaze on His beautiful face.
All things of earth will disappear
When we behold His glory.

In this life we will be disappointed.
We will be hurt by the ones we love.
But if God is our Father and Lord,
We will ultimately gain His reward.

Psalm of Prayer For Redemption

Lord of mercy, God of love,
Hear my prayer today.
My soul is distressed within me.
For I have sinned greatly against You.

I fell into a trap,
So carefully laid by Satan.
He knew my weakest places
To form his strategy and attack.

He knew I was so tired
Both physically and emotionally.
He knew I would be an easy mark,
Too weak to fight him off.

My great love for my family
And the strength they gave to me
Was the spot he marked to attack.
And with vengeance, he took over my life.

My emotions were his first attack.
I was already lower than low.
All I wanted was to escape;
To be free of all in this world.

My brain, the source of intellect,
Was attacked with hatred and vengeance.
He invaded both waking and sleeping
With thoughts of unspeakable rage.

I could not sleep for his viciousness.
There was no rest for even a minute.
Thoughts I hated myself for thinking,
Left me too broken and tired to resist.

He found the very weakest point
In my heart that had been broken.
The pain of believing my world was destroyed
Gave him plenty of ammunition.

My emotions were out of control;
I could do nothing but weep.
But he kept coming stronger each day
With more depression and anxiety.

Barbs of hate were thrown at me.
All I heard spoke only of abandonment.
No mercy or compassion were sent my way--
Only assaults against my heart.

Then came the anger and need for revenge.
I had to get back at those who hurt me.
If I could hurt others the way I had been hurt,
Then just maybe I would feel better.

I could see no one who cared enough
To come to my defense.
I had to protect myself from the onslaught
Even if it meant losing everything.

Never once did Satan let up.
His attacks grew more vicious by the day.
He was getting just what he had planned--
The destruction of love and family.

I had lost everything that I held dear
When my defeat was definite and clear.
All my hopes and dreams had been crushed,
And I was the one who did it.

I was so depressed and downtrodden.
My body was physically ill.
All I wanted was to be released
While Satan was gloating and laughing.

In all the time I was being deceived,
Lord, You never left me.
Even when I shook my fist in your face
And cried that I had been abandoned.

As I begged for forgiveness,
Ever so slowly Your light returned.
But then the guilt of what I had done
Crashed into my heart and soul.

Another attack by the enemy,
Told me I was too evil for forgiveness.
The hatefulness and anger that spewed out of my mouth
Could never be redeemed.

Excuses appeared one after one.
I had been hurt and broken in two.
I was provoked with hateful lies
And betrayed by those I loved.

There was no excuse for what I had done.
I had let Satan take over my soul.
Over my thoughts, my words, and emotions,
I had given him full control.

What have I done, O God?
How could I let myself fall?
The wiles of Satan took over the soul
Of a life I had committed to You.

Oh Lord, hear my prayer. I have sinned against You.
I have committed sins so grievous I cannot bear to recall.
I was blinded by Satan so easily.
I am ashamed and guilty before You.

You have heard my groans and seen my tears.
You know the despair of my heart.
You, waiting patiently for me to return,
Had been there all the time.

I cry out to You, Lord,
Forgive my foolishness.
Restore unto me the joy of my salvation
Create a clean heart in me.

O Father on high, Almighty Lord,
Take my sins and cast them away.
Fill the brokenness and despair in my soul
With the presence of Your Spirit.

I ask You to restore what has been broken and ravaged
Only Your Hand has the power to do it.
Nothing on this earth I could ever say or do
Can make up for my mistakes.

Turn my weeping into joy.
Fill my emptiness with Your love.
Open my eyes to see Your grace.
Cleanse my heart with Your gracious mercy.

Clothe me with Your armor, God,
Give me eyes of discernment.
Teach me how to repel Satan's darts;
How to fight with the tools You have given.

Thank You God, I praise Your name
For what You are doing for me.
I feel Your presence and Your love
Working to heal my soul.

I love You Lord. I give You my life.
I place everything in Your hands.
No other would welcome me with open arms.
I have been the prodigal one.

Psalm of Fear

We see fear all around us,
Everywhere we look.
Fear of the loss of earthly things
Binds us to the darkness.

All trouble stems from fear.
Wars are caused by fear.
Relationships are ruined by fear.
Hatred stems from fear.

Fear is the root of all negative emotions.
Yet, we let fear govern our lives.
Anger, anxiety, depression, and envy
Are all based on our fears of loss.

We are taught by the world we live in
To be afraid of losing.
We cling with all our might
To the things that make us feel secure.

We learn as children to be afraid for ourselves.
We are punished when we do wrong.
As we grow, we keep that fear
And let it grow stronger and stronger.

We fear losing our security
Provided by jobs and money.
We are bound to earthly things
In order to get more and more.

The fear of losing relationships
Leads to jealousy and bickering.
Gossip that kills the spirit
Is another manifestation.

We strive to cling so tightly
To things we consider ours.
We will do whatever it takes
To keep them for ourselves.

We do not want to give up anything,
That we fear will affect our lifestyle.
We must show the world we are prospering
By what we do and all we have.

Keeping up with the Joneses
Becomes our number one goal.
We are so afraid of losing the acceptance of society
That we put ourselves in debt to maintain our image.

Fear and worry go hand in hand,
Even though God told us not to worry.
Fear and worry about tomorrow
Binds our thoughts and our freedom.

Most people even fear our God.
They worry they are not good enough.
We have been taught to see God
As vengeful and unforgiving.

Fear is not from God!
God's love looks past our sin.
He corrects us with His overwhelming love
And gives His unconditional forgiveness.

Fear is a tool of Satan
To keep us from the freedom of true love.
He keeps us bound to him
By making us fear loss and grief.

There is no fear in love.[29]
God's perfect love casts out fear.
When we let go of the fear in our lives,
We become free to enjoy true love.

Psalm of My Life

I have lived many years on this earth.
I have seen good, and I have seen bad.
I have experienced things that could have destroyed me
And taken away everything good.

I have been lied to and lied about.
Things that broke my heart in two.
I have been bullied and put down
And threatened with bodily pain.

I have been laughed at and made fun of
And told hurtful things by others.
Trying to make me ashamed of who I am.
So I will run and hide away.

I have been used, and I have been abused
By words and actions that could have haunted me forever.
I have been accused of awful things
By people filled with hatred and jealousy.

I have been fired from jobs I have loved
Because of who I am.
I have been discriminated against
Because I am a woman, not a man.

Promises have been broken.
Life has not been fair or kind.
Sickness and death of family and loved ones alike
Have all been part of my life.

I have watched children fight and die
From diseases they do not deserve.
There has been tragedy in my family.
There are things I still do not understand.

I have had no money, and I have had plenty,
I have been homeless and had a fine home.
I have been denied many things I wanted
But never have I been alone.

Depression and despair have plagued me.
There were times I wanted to give up.
There were times when I was not sure of anything
Except the pain I felt in my heart.

Yet, in all these times of sorrow,
There is one thing of which I am sure.
I am the daughter of the Most High God,
And nothing on earth can destroy me.

I also have committed countless sins.
Many have grieved the heart of God.
I have fallen on my face in repentance
And cried for forgiveness and grace.

I have shed many tears of sorrow and pain--
More than I could ever count.
I have wondered at times where God was
When my heart was filled with doubt.

In anger and desperation
I have shaken my fist in His face.
But He has never let me go.
He loved me despite myself.

Each day I have joy in Him
Despite all the world has done.
I can stand in the midst of trouble.
My victory has already been won.

No lies, abuse, or depression,
Can change who I am in my Father.
Even though men might kill this body,
I am eternally alive in Him.

There is nothing I would change in my life
Even though some things still bring pain.
In everything I have been through,
I have come out stronger than before.

God has blessed me richly
With family, friends, and possessions.
He has provided everything I need
To live happily and joyfully forever.

I have had laughter and fun and happiness
Even among the things that hurt.
I have had joy in Christ my Savior,
Though life was sometimes cruel.

I have experienced excitement and awe of the Lord,
As I have looked in the faces of my children and grandchildren.
I have cherished each moment with them--
These blessings that God has given.

I could choose to live my life
Haunted by things that have happened.
I could be miserable and unforgiving,
Only hurting myself.

I choose to live in contentment,
The contentment that comes from God.
I have the peace and light in my soul
That can only come from Him.

God assures me every day I live
That nothing can change who I am.
Though troubles may come and go,
In Christ I am made worthy.

I am worthy of love and blessing,
Worthy of the blood of the Lamb,
Worthy to be forgiven of sins;
Worthy of life eternal.

I refuse to let this world defeat me.
I will not let Satan win!
There is nothing this world can do to me
That God will not work for good in the end.

I praise You God for my life
And everything I have been through--
For my many years of joy and strife,
And for the love I feel in You.

I do not know how my days have been appointed.[30]
You have my life in Your hands.
For however much longer I have on this earth,
In Your strength I will take my stand.

I will tell of Your love and mercy,
Of Your faithfulness, and of Your blessings.
I will lift my praise to You
Until my life has ended.

Psalm of Doubt

When I wake up in the morning,
I look at myself in the mirror.
I see lines and wrinkles of age,
And I doubt anyone could love me.

As I go about my daily chores,
I am discouraged by all I do.
I doubt anyone cares enough to visit.
So, why waste my time and effort?

I go out to run my errands,
The things that must be done.
I want to hide myself away.
Doubt says no one wants to see me.

Doubt creeps into my mind
When I study the Word of God.
I am too old to memorize Scripture.
I doubt it matters anyway.

Preparing to teach my classes,
I keep thinking how useless it is.
I doubt any student will listen.
Why should I even try?

When my child does not call to check in,
I feel I have failed as a mother.
I doubt that he even loves me.
I must have done everything wrong.

I look around me and see
A world filled with chaos and hatred.
Everything seems to be going wrong,
And I have doubts about the future.

I doubt that God hears my prayers.
It seems they go no higher than the ceiling.
I doubt that He really cares about me
Because I do not see Him working.

I feel I am being consumed by doubts.
It has led me to despair.
I think I am not good enough to live.
I doubt anyone would miss me.

Doubt can take over a life.
It is a seed planted by Satan.
When a person allows doubt to enter his heart,
It grows stronger and stronger and stronger.

Doubt creeps in when my faith is weak.
It will not leave me alone.
But what does God say to me about doubt?
He is the final authority.

God says I am beautiful.
He loves me just the way I am.
God never looks on the outside,
But sees who I am within.

God knows my heart even more than I do.
He loves to banish my doubts.
He assures me He hears every prayer I pray,
Even when I cannot see Him working.

Everything that comes my way,
Is filtered through God's hand.
He will not let me be destroyed
By doubt and lack of faith.

He builds me up and restores my faith.
His Spirit moves within me.
I can be sure of His love and grace
No matter what assails me.

We must trust in the Lord with all our heart.[31]
Do not lean to our own understanding.
For the understanding of man is flawed
And does not seek the heart of God.

We must call on Him in faith
With no doubt or fear within us.
For if we doubt God's power,
We become confused and torn by the world.

I am determined to live my life
Without doubt or despair or confusion.
I will trust in the God who made me
And believe He works for my good.

God will fulfill His purpose in my life.
He ordained it from the beginning.
His steadfast love endures forever.
He will equip me with all I need.

When doubt creeps into my heart,
So subtle I do not recognize it.
I will declare that it is defeated
By the precious blood of Jesus

SECTION 7

PSALMS OF LIVING
IN CHRIST

Psalm For the Believer

Hold tight, O saint, hold tight
To the presence in you of the Spirit.
Hold tight to the love of your Father
And the knowledge that you are His child.

When troubles come, and they will,
Hold tight to the power of your God.
He created you with His hand.
He will never allow you to fall.

His love for you is fierce
Like a lioness protecting her cubs.
He will destroy all your enemies
And bring you safely home.

He is reckless in His pursuit.
He goes with you into the fire.
Never alone will you be in distress.
His infinite love will find you there.

When you are weak, He is strong.
When you are in trouble, He is your comfort.
When you doubt, He is your truth.
And when you are dying, He is your life.

This overwhelming love of God
You think you do not deserve.
Yet, He gave away His life for you
To make you worthy through grace.

He has already forgiven your sin.
He mends you when you fail.
He has made your life brand new.
His mercy exceeds all bounds.

Hold fast to the truth of His grace.
You can never outlive His love.
He is faithful at all times and in all ways.
He is your Lord and King.

He is the life, the truth, the way[32]
Even when you think you are lost.
Hold His promises deep in your heart
And His Word in your mind always.

So, hold tight, dear saint, hold tight.
There is nothing to worry or fear.
When God is the light of your life,
Your way will be blessed and clear.

The path you travel on earth will get hard,
But joy He will give to your soul.
Have faith and trust in Him alone.
Do not let darkness have control.

No one could love you more
Than God your Father on high.
He holds you tight in His mighty hand.
He will never let you go.

Praise His name, dear saint, for you are loved.
Lift your hands to Him in thanksgiving.
Honor His name in all things
And sing His praises forever.

Psalm of Living

Live through me Lord, live through me.
Place Your Spirit in my life that all may ever see.
Put your hand upon my life to reach out to set them free
As You live through me.

Speak through me Lord, speak through me.
Let my lips become Your mouthpiece speaking confidently.
Give me words that will speak life to all who hear of Thee
As you speak through me.

Touch through me Lord, touch through me.
Give me hands to reach the hurting to give them the key
Of comfort, peace, and presence found in trusting Thee
As You touch through me.

Walk through me Lord, walk through me.
Lead my steps to those who need You; lead them steadfastly.
Show me the path to take that points the way to Thee
As You walk through me.

Psalm of Mission

There are so many times
When I do not know what to do.
Solutions and answers
Do not seem to come through.

The right words to say and the way to speak
Are contrary to my basest instincts.
I grapple with situations and circumstances
That are so foreign to me.

There are those against me,
Whose beliefs are different than mine;
Those who refuse to listen
When the truth is there all the time.

Many accuse me of using my faith
To benefit only myself.
Those held in bondage to addiction
Are unable to see beyond themselves.

I see those, through no fault of their own,
Who are living in poverty and grief.
Others are living with evil intentions
While disregarding goodness and light.

What is my mission to these
And so many more around me?
How can I minister to people in need--
To those who need to know God's love?

When evil words are hurled at me,
When my faith is pummeled and maligned,
When others laugh and call me a fraud,
I will deny their attempts to destroy my peace.

How can I help those who abuse me?
How can I love without judgment
When my heart is broken and tears flow freely?
How can I show them the true way of life?

LOVE whether it is deserved or not.
LOVE when I do not find it justified.
LOVE through hurt, anger, and disappointment.
LOVE all, no matter the circumstances!

LOVE God first.
LOVE your neighbor as yourself.
LOVE all who have much or nothing.
LOVE everyone, everywhere, every time!

LOVE amidst being maligned.
LOVE even when it takes all your will.
LOVE those who abuse and curse you.
LOVE with the love of God!

Give to the needy with LOVE.
Minister to those who are hurting with LOVE.
When words are not received, show LOVE.
When you do not know what to do, just LOVE.

The love of God shown through me
Is the reality that fulfills every hope.
Showing the love that triumphs over all things
Is the way to reach others for Him.

Psalm of Obedience

Thousands of years ago,
The world had grown very evil.
Sin, flaunted in the face of God,
Was running rampant.

God called upon a man,
The only one who served the Lord,
To build an ark for a coming flood,
And Noah obeyed.

Not one was saved from the flooded earth,
But Noah and his family.
Through Noah, God gave man another chance
To serve the one true Lord.

Many years later it happened again.
God's people became sinful and disobedient.
God turned them over to their enemies
To be slaves to the Egyptians.

For 200 years they served as slaves,
Ruled over by harsh taskmasters.
God called a man to lead them out,
And Moses obeyed.

From slaves to free people, blessed by God again,
The people were promised a land
Flowing with milk and honey--
Another place for them to start over.

Because of their disobedience,
This land would not be free.
They must fight to gain what was promised,
But He assured them victory.

Many kingdoms were toppled by the people of God.
Their obedience gave them success.
They trusted in God's plan to win the land
In impossible circumstances.

In a strategy to win part of the promised land,
God called on a leader of the people.
He said, 'March around the wall and blow your horns,"
And Joshua obeyed.

Yet, once again after being so blessed,
Man turned away from God.
God sent men to warn them of captivity,
And the prophets obeyed.

Even after being warned so many times,
The people kept sinning before God.
Their stubbornness and arrogance
Kept leading them to destruction.

Yet, God so loved the world,[33]
And His creation of mankind,
That He made a way for all people to be saved,
And Jesus, His Son, obeyed.

Giving His life for the sins of the world,
Our Messiah and Savior He became.
He took the sins of all mankind
On Himself that we might be delivered.

Over and over the people of God
Have turned to sin and rebellion.
Our longsuffering God gives us chance after chance,
Reminding us to be obedient.

In all of history time after time,
God has called His people back to Himself.
Yet we, His crowing creation,
Return to our sinful ways.

Obedience to the commands of God
Is what brings us blessing from Him.
We must turn from our wicked ways
And repent of all our sins.

God blesses the people who are true to His word.
He has given them His promise.
All He requires is obedience in love
To claim His mercy and forgiveness.

Psalm on Micah 6: 8

What do You require of me Lord?
You have done so much for me.
How can I ever repay You
For the sacrifice You made for all men?

There is not anything I can do
That is worthy of Your love.
Nothing in my finite mind
Can conceive of how to glorify You.

I look to Your Holy Word
To learn how I can honor You.
What You require from me is so simple.
Yet, it seems not enough to do.

I must walk humbly with God always[34]
And seek every day to glorify Him.
Seek His will and His way
In everything I do and say.

I pray, Lord, for meekness and modesty
So that my visage would reflect Your glory.
Help me never give or do for my own reward
Only because You first gave to me.

Let me act justly toward all people and
Hold no grievance or bias toward others.
Show me how to be upright and pure in my dealings,
Never partial, unjust, or unfitting.

Lord, let me be Your instrument
To minister to others for You.
Let me show them the justice and mercy
You give so freely to me.

Teach me to have mercy for all humanity and
To be compassionate and full of grace.
I seek to show charity, generosity, and blessing,
In my words, in my deeds, and on my face.

Father, let my life be an example
Of the grace and mercy You give.
May my heart be filled with kindness
Toward others who are in need.

May everything, I think, say, and do
Work only for Your glory.
Take my life, my breath, my heart, my soul,
As a living sacrifice to You.

Now justice, mercy, and humbleness,
Are how we can honor our God.
The way to a righteous life on earth
Is shown by Jesus our Lord.

Psalm on The Fruit of The Spirit

Holy Spirit fill my life;
Teach me how to live
In a world of darkness and sin.
Let Your glory reflect in my countenance.

In sorrow, in pain, in trouble, and despair
Give me joy beyond measure in Thee.
Let my life reflect Your light
To all who might seek comfort.

Grant me joy unspeakable and full of glory[35]
That lifts burdens and dispels all sorrow--
The joy that can only come through You,
Shining in me for others to see.

With the love of the Almighty
Fill my heart, my soul, my mind.
Give me love for all around me
No matter who they are.

Teach me love without condition,
Love that forgives all things.
Let me see all things through Your eyes;
Never judge nor condemn.

Send the peace that passes understanding[36]
In everything that confronts me.
My mind will rest in Thee
No matter what dangers beset me.

I need peace that You are with me,
Peace in the battles of life.
The peace that only You can give
Reigns in my heart through trouble and strife.

Let kindness toward others around me
Give me purpose and ministry.
May my motives be filled with gentleness
That others will see Jesus in me.

Oh, that goodness would be my credo,
And grace would fill my heart.
So that the righteousness given to me
Can be seen in my actions and words.

Give me patience, Father, to know
That not all things are for my good.
Help me to wait for Your voice to speak;
To do the things I should.

I pray that the gentleness of Jesus
Would saturate my soul and my heart.
I ask that I would never judge or hurt
In my deeds, my words, or my thoughts.

Help me to keep check on my motives.
Show me how to exercise self-control.
Let everything that comes to my mind
Sift through Your filter of love.

Integrity and virtue are the marks of a godly person.
Dignity and morality are to be held up for display.
My life cannot be what You will, O Lord,
Without the guidance of Your Spirit.

Psalm of God's First Command

Love the Lord your God
With all your heart and being.[37]
Then, love others as yourself
Is the greatest command.

Let us all love one another
As commanded by God himself.
May we have compassionate hearts
To love all those around us.

Our hearts have become hard and calloused.
The world's standard drives us to immovability.
Give me a new heart formed by You, Lord,
With love as its ultimate purpose.

Help me to love the hardest to love.
Take away any prejudice in me.
Put away the things I have believed in the past
Taught to me by society.

I must look through the eyes of faith
To be able to love all people.
No matter what race, creed, or religion,
They are all God's children.

All over the world evil is spreading.
Hatred and revenge rage wild.
World governments killing children and families,
Are common everyday news.

Lord, it is so hard to love people,
Who deliberately set out to hurt others--
Especially ones who persecute Your children,
Who try to put Christianity to an end.

Yet, You created these people as well,
Just the same as You created me.
They, too, are Your children on earth,
Though they deny all knowledge of You.

Hearts have foolishly turned from You,
Turned to other gods and idols.
Love is now a weak emotion
Frowned upon by the masses.

This heart in my earthly body
Is not capable of loving like You.
Give me a new heart, dear Lord,
That reflects Your love.

Loving one another is the only answer
To ending all hatred and malice.
God, You knew from the beginning
True love is the only way.

So, many thousands of years ago,
You told us how to live.
Your infinite wisdom, written by Your own hand:
Love God first, and then love one another.

Put away all pre-conceived notions
Of self-righteous indignation.
Put away the standard of the world.
Love first, as God commanded.

Psalm of Discouragement

Lord, it is so easy to get discouraged
When things are not going my way.
It is easy to blame it all on You
Because You control all things.

It is so hard to understand
Some of the things that happen.
Could they possibly come from You
And be used for good in Your plan?

When things or people turn against me,
My heart gets confused and broken.
It is so easy to just stop praying
And stop depending on You.

Things do not always turn out
The way I expected them to.
It seems like You never answer
As I pour out my heart to You.

When my faith is tested and persecuted,
When I feel the pressure of others,
When I am feeling so vulnerable,
I question all I believe.

When I cannot feel Your presence,
In those times I feel so alone;
When hurt and sorrow are all I can feel,
It is tempting to step out on my own.

Lord, I try to remember Your promise
Given to me in Your Word.
"In this world you will have trouble,[38]
But fear not, I have overcome."

You knew how hard it would be
To live in a world full of sin.
You told me to depend on You
That I might have peace within.

I know that You are with me
Even when I am discouraged.
I know You understand how I feel
When tears flow from my soul.

Thank you, Lord, for Your Word
Spoken to give me courage.
Just like an earthly parent, but more,
You empathize with my struggles.

When my tears flow so do Yours.
When I feel punched in the gut, You do too.
There is nothing that happens to me
That You have not felt before.

Lord, give me strength to live in this world
Where evil is out to consume me.
Let me always remember Your Word;
To be strong and stand to fight.

Turn my discouragement into joy
By the power of your Spirit.
Give me the strength I need
To overcome the world.

Psalm of Things I Have Learned in My Life

~

Throughout the decades of my life,
Many lessons have been learned.
Looking back over the years,
I wonder at all I have experienced.

People on this earthly plain
Are fallible and imperfect.
Sometimes without intention
We will disappoint or hurt others.

No one can be fully trusted
To do and act as they say.
Excuses are easily given
To justify actions and mistakes.

There is only one in whom we can implicitly trust--
Only one who makes no mistakes.
His Word has been infallible for thousands of years.
Not one word or action is false.

What God says, He will do.
What He promises can be expected.
The things He gives, He gives to all.
His honor is intractable.

The word of mankind no longer has merit.
A little white lie is not a sin.
So what, if we break our promises?
Hurting others is no big deal.

I have learned that the tongues God gave us
Can be treacherous and very evil.
Words can cause devastating wounds
To those we love the most.

Words of judgment and hate,
Words of anger and retribution,
Words that tear families and friendships apart,
Are so easily spoken.

In my life, I have hurt others
With words I wish I could recall.
I, too, have been hurt by ones
Whose words have ripped my soul.

God warns us to keep a check on everything we say;
To be mindful of every word.
We must guard our tongues before we speak
So that our words do not kill a spirit.

I have learned that everything I do
Always has a consequence.
Life is filled with choices we make;
Those choices determine our lives.

We do not have the wisdom
To see the results of our choices.
Something we think will be good for us
Can bring evil upon another.

God has made a way for us
To know the right choices to make.
His Spirit living within our souls
Can guide and direct our actions.

His Word gives us direction.
He has always known the right way.
His wisdom sees all that ever was,
That is, and that ever will be.

I have learned that life is like a race.
How I run it determines my place.
To run the race well, I must look to God
For the stamina and strength to keep going.

I must fight the good fight every day of my life
So that I will be proven acceptable.
Using God's Word to search out His will,
I have the strength and conviction to win.

There is too much pain and sorrow
In this world in which I live.
I cannot survive it all on my own.
I must lean and depend on Him.

Peace is a gift from God;
Not the peace that the world gives.
The peace of the world is fleeting.
It will not stand in the face of trouble.

The deep abiding peace in my soul
Is God's gift that carries me through.
It is there in every circumstance
And never leaves me alone.

Above all, love is the essential way
To live a life of joy.
Love for self and all of God's children,
Is shown in the life of Jesus.

I must speak and act in the love of Christ.
I must forgive and not hold grievances.
I must strive to see everyone through His eyes of love
And give with no thought of receiving.

So many lessons I have learned.
Yet, I am learning still.
God give me a hunger to seek Your will
Until You take me home.

Psalm of Promises

We live in a time where promises
Mean little if anything.
We have come to expect a promise
Or word of another to be broken.

From childhood we learn the concept
That a promise should always be kept.
Early in life we begin to believe
A promise is going to happen.

Children beg parents to promise
To give them something they want.
They learn trust and belief in others
Based on promises broken or kept.

Couples make promises in marriage
To love and forsake all others.
A vow is to be kept for a lifetime,
But so many times it is broken.

Friendships are based on a promise
That we will always support each other.
We can each depend on the other
To be there in time of need.

We hear and see promises every day
From advertisers and social media.
They promise to make our lives better
If only we buy their product.

Most promises have become empty.
They are only words to fit the occasion.
Words just placate another
Into believing we mean what we say.

Promises made mean nothing
If it proves inconvenient for us.
"I know I promised, but something came up."
Another commitment is broken.

What is a promise broken
If not a word of dishonesty?
To say that we will keep our word
Is often simply not true.

We have become a society of lies
Where our word means nothing.
Trust is no longer respected.
Honesty no longer admired.

Promises to children are broken.
Marriage vows rarely are kept.
Friendships dissolve in betrayal.
And yet, there is no regret.

Promises by business and advertisers
Are mostly made to deceive us.
All they want is our money
With no thought of a guarantee.

In this day of no respect,
When our word is no longer our bond,
Greed and selfishness abound
And mean more than any promise.

There is one who we can depend on
Whose every word is true.
There is one who will not let us down
In any circumstance.

Our Father God who made us
Made promises to His children.
Never once in all of history
Have those promises He forsaken.

We can always and forever
Depend on His every Word.
His love for us is unshakable.
His promises strong and true.

Every promise He has made
Will be kept throughout all time.
We are the recipients of
His infallible, intractable Word.

He promises life eternal
As proof that we will never be alone.
He promises to defend us
Against evil that would destroy.

He promised to meet our needs,
To hear our every prayer;
To make a way of escape
When temptation overcomes us.

Always and forever He will comfort us
When our hearts are torn and broken.
He hears our every cry
When pain is all we know.

So many promises He makes,
All for our well-being,
To help us live in a world of sin;
To give us peace unending.

The promise of eternal life
Is offered to each person.
An eternal home with Him in heaven
Is prepared for those who love Him.

O God, we praise and thank You
That Your promises are eternal.
No matter what we experience in life,
You alone can always be trusted.

Psalm of The Power of Words

Words are expressions of ourselves
To give us a way to let others know us.
Words give meaning to our feelings.
They allow us to communicate.

Millions of words are used every day
For many varied purposes.
We use so many words in life
That we cannot keep track of them.

Instruction is given to others
With words of academia.
We learn to use them properly;
To be understood in their meaning.

From babies to adulthood
We learn to use our words.
To become fluent in our language
On many different levels.

Children learn the words they use
From parents and others around them.
Some learn words they should not know--
Words too harsh for their tender spirits.

Words can be beneficial.
They can be beautiful and eloquent.
They can be simple or hard to understand.
They can be hurtful and heart breaking.

Our lives can be enriched by words
When used to benefit others.
They can build us up and make us feel good,
But words can also destroy us.

Words are hurled in anger
With no thought of consequence.
Words of scorn and contempt are uttered
Against those with whom we disagree.

Words of hate and judgment are spoken
Against ones we see as wrong.
Words can be as deadly as a gun or knife.
They can kill the spirit.

Wars are caused by words
Between people whose beliefs differ.
Threats, disdain, and derision
Can cause the destruction of nations.

Words we use so casually
Often can be misinterpreted.
Our meaning may be totally innocent,
But wrong interpretations can be disastrous.

The words used by adults around children
Will be remembered the rest of their lives.
Children absorb everything they hear.
Our words may determine their future.

Words of love give us wonderful feelings.
They make us believe we are worthy.
Affirmation given to others
Always bring them closer to us.

Kindness and compassion,
Expressed to those in need
Coupled with words of concern we can reach them
And give their life meaning.

Words, the most common of everyday things,
Can take on a life of their own.
The way they are used by each person
Can bring life or death to the soul.

Words can be a terrible weapon.
They can hurt, destroy, and kill.
Words once uttered from our mouth
Can never be taken back.

God Himself has instructed us
To consider each word we utter.
Evil can be housed in the tongue
But so can mercy and love.

There are many idioms
We are urged to use in life.
Think before you speak is one.
Use your words only for good is another.

Others urge us to be kind;
To never speak in anger.
"If you cannot say something nice,
Do not say anything at all."

Nevertheless, words are taken
Into our spirit and our soul.
We may be able to forgive them,
But they will never be forgotten.

Jesus gave us an example,
Of how all words should be used.
Only in truth and love
Should any words ever be spoken.

Build up others in love.
Never tear them down.
Do not use words to hurt or harm.
Never use them to gossip.

The words we use are a witness
Of whom we truly are.
Our lives are viewed by others
As a product of what we say.

We have all used words inappropriately.
We have all hurt others inadvertently.
We must stop and take into consideration
How our words can sound to others.

We must use the example of Christ
To fix a world that is broken.
Instead of anger, hurt, and judgment
Use our words as weapons of peace.

Psalm of Choice

We always have a choice
In deciding which way to go.
In everything we encounter, we choose
The things we say and do.

From the time we are children,
We learn to make choices.
The correct behavior gets praise,
But the wrong behavior is punished.

Parents teach their little ones
The difference between right and wrong.
All throughout our lives,
We make choices which define us.

Society gives us rules and laws
That we choose to follow or break.
We have been indoctrinated by government
To choose the right or the left.

Many times we struggle
To choose the best way to go.
Doing what is good and true
Is often overshadowed by wrong.

God tells us to be incredibly careful
In choosing how to live our lives.
There is a way that seems right to man
That leads to death in the end.[39]

In all our knowledge and wisdom
The selfishness of man takes over.
We do what we believe makes us happy.
God's way is never considered.

God's Word tells us plainly,
Do not enter the way of the wicked.[40]
When we choose to do what is evil,
Our lives are consumed by sin.

Crooked and perverse paths
Will only lead to destruction.
While the right, the just, and the truthful
Will lead to everlasting life.

The way of the just is light,
But the way of evil is dark.
Every moment we live we choose
To live in the darkness or light.

Our choices define our lives.
We live either for God or the world.
Our future is determined
By the path we choose each day.

God's eyes are everywhere.
He sees our every choice.
He lovingly calls us to right and truth,
But the choice is ours to make.

Psalm of Time

Time is so crucial
To our daily lives.
It comes and goes relentlessly,
Never considering what we want.

So often we say we do not have enough time.
If only there were more hours in the day,
We could do so much more to meet our needs;
Accomplish what we think is important.

Watches, clocks, calendars, and planners:
We must have them at the ready.
We cannot function if things are not timed
To fit our busy schedule.

Hurry here, hurry there--
We must keep up with the clock.
There is no time to sit down and rest.
We fill our brains with deadlines.

We stay busy, busy, busy.
We must do this and that.
There is not enough time in the day
To do anything else that matters.

We must fill every hour with busyness,
Down to the very last minute
In order to be productive in life;
To be a success in society.

What is time in the scheme of all things?
Why have we made it so important?
Why must we live on a schedule
And wear ourselves out in the process?

Time is a method created by man,
To measure the passage of nature.
Day, night, seasons, and years
Come and go in our concept of time.

But in God's time, there is no clock.
A thousand years are only a blink of His eye.
The concept of time we have adopted
Is foreign to His plan.

Time as we know it is only an illusion--
A way to account for what we do.
But what we do with our time here on earth
Is what matters in the end.

Man's days on earth will come to an end
Sooner than we may like.
We do not know the day or time.
Yet, every person will see death.

God has provided a way
That eternity can be ours.
It is not the time we know on earth
But an unending life of joy.

Time will not be filled
With rushing and watching a clock or
Doing things that are meaningless
In God's eternal plan.

The blood of Jesus, shed for us,
Gives us unending access to God.
Accepting Him as Savior and Lord
Makes time take on a new meaning.

The things we do here in our days on earth
Will have no meaning in the end
Unless we are doing the things of God
As He meant for us from the beginning.

Psalm of Courage

Child of God do not be afraid
Of the evil that stalks our land.
Stand strong in God's might, His power, and promise
To deliver you from Satan's plan.

Nothing or no one can remove God's hand
That was on you before your birth.
No temptation or evil can destroy you
When by His hand you are covered.

He provides a way to escape
The temptation that comes upon you.
You have the power of the Holy Spirit in you
To command Satan to leave your presence.

Satan has no power over you.
He can only invade if you let him.
Though temptations assault you day after day,
You can stand strong in the might of the Lord.

Satan will use every tool he can;
Even people you think you can trust.
He finds the weakest spot in your heart;
Then attacks with vengeance and hatred.

Put on the armor God has given you.
We find it in His Word.
Rest in the knowledge He has given
That you are not alone in the fight.

Be strong and courageous. Do not fear the battle.
You are one of God's own.
You have the power of heaven behind you
With all the might it holds.

You have been set free from evil intentions
By the blood of Jesus your Savior.
Take shelter and rest under His mighty wings.
He will never leave or forsake you.

Dear child of God do not be afraid.
The victory is already yours.
God's promise to be with you is strong and true.
He never fails His children.

Psalm of Assurance

How do you smile
When you are burying a loved one?
How do you smile
When troubles hit your life?

How do you smile
When you face financial ruin?
How do you smile
When your child goes astray?

How do you smile
When others set out to destroy you?
How do you smile
Amidst gossip that kills your soul?

How do you smile
When your family is divided?
How do you smile
When an accident takes your child?

There is only one way
To live when life seems hopeless.
There is only one way
To survive among the thorns.

There is only one way
To have peace in all your troubles.
There is only one way
To find joy amidst the storms.

You can thrive in times of trouble
When your faith is in the Lord.
You can smile in all your heartbreak
When your joy comes from the Lord.

You can rest when storms surround you
When you believe His Word.
You can be at peace when you are maligned
When you know He is at your side.

God told us in His Word that
In this life we would have troubles.
He showed us in His Word
We would be shunned by those we love.

He revealed in His Word
We would be persecuted.
He assured us in His Word
We could stand firm against the world.

God promised not to leave us,
Nor ever to forsake us.
He promised to give us joy
When we put our trust in Him.

He said He would send His comfort
When our hearts are totally breaking.
He promised to send peace
When we feel we are in a war.

All we must do
Is believe in His promise.
We must trust that He is true
And steadfast in His love.

We take Him at His Holy Word and
Believe that He will save us.
We claim His joy and love and peace
To have complete contentment.

We will not fear what happens
Or be anxious for tomorrow.
We place our faith in Him
To provide the help we need.

We know that there is a better place
Where troubles will not exist.
This life we are living now
Is not our final home.

We will be with Him forever.
We will be reunited with our loved ones.
There will be no sickness, toil, or strife
In the place that He has prepared.

How do we smile through troubles,
Pain, and loss of things in life?
We know within our hearts and minds
We have salvation in Jesus Christ.

Psalm of Forgiveness

Forgiving is something
That is extremely hard to do.
It goes against our instincts
And what we are taught by the world.

We are hurt by those we trust;
Ones we give our love to.
We are hurt by people
Who do not care how they hurt others.

Whether physical or emotional,
The pain we feel is real.
Whether accidental or intentional,
Anger at the offender is what we feel.

When we are betrayed by others,
Justice is what we crave.
We must get even with the offender
No matter what it costs.

But God says we must forgive,
Up to seventy times seven.[41]
No matter the insult or hurt,
We must be willing to forgive.

Why should we forgive
When we have been so hurt?
Why should we forgive an offense
When we are not the offender?

Unforgiveness becomes a toxin,
Wreaking havoc in our minds.
Our hearts are overtaken
By bitterness and rage.

Our mind keeps replaying the incident
Over and over and over.
Offense takes over every thought,
Destroying our peace and trust.

We become more bitter and angry
With every day that passes.
Our sleep and rest are troubled
By dreams of anger and rage.

Emotions become brittle
And sometimes out of control.
It is as if a sickness is growing
In our minds and in our souls.

Unforgiveness drags us down
Like an anchor around our neck.
We must fight harder every day
Just to stay afloat.

Everything we do or say
Is overshadowed by our anger.
Everything we think or feel
Is mirrored in our hurt.

What are we to do
When bitterness is destroying us?
How can we stop this downward slide
Into anger and mistrust?

Forgiveness is the only cure
To give us peace and joy.
When we forgive, the infection in our soul
Begins to melt away.

Yet, forgiveness seems impossible
When we look at the offense.
How could someone do this to me
And hurt me so grievously?

We want to get away;
Never see the offender again.
We want to cut them off
From everything we do.

But unforgiveness binds us to the person
Who hurt and offended us.
We give them the power to destroy our peace
And fill us with misery and depression.

Yet, forgiving is one of the hardest things
We will ever have to do.
On our own we do not have grace enough
To forgive completely.

God alone has the grace and power
To forgive every offense.
We must first give our hurt to Him
To bring forgiveness into our heart.

If we want to be forgiven
When we sin, as every person does,
God says we must first forgive others,
So that He then can forgive us.

Harboring unforgiveness in our heart
Binds the forgiveness and grace of God,
Our anger, bitterness, and hurt,
Keep us from receiving His peace.

We should learn from Jesus
Who set the ultimate example.
When He was betrayed, abused, and killed,
His cry was, "Father forgive them."[42]

Forgiveness sets us free.
It allows healing in our heart.
Letting go of all the bitterness
Makes room for peace and love.

Yes, forgiveness sets us free, but we can never forget
The wrongs, the hurts, and the offenses against us.
Our finite minds do not have the capability
To forget the trauma in life.

The memory will always stay
Until we determine to put it away.
True forgiveness requires treating the offense
As if it never happened.

We must do as Jesus did that day
When He gave us forgiveness from sin.
He forgave our sin and cast it away
As far as the east is from the west.

It is so difficult in this world
To cast away wrongdoings.
Sometimes we must continue to forgive
Day after day after day.

Satan will try to remind us of the offense
In our mind and in our heart.
He puts it back into our thoughts
For as long as we will let him.

It takes all our strength to determine to forgive.
It will take all our fortitude.
We must fight the battle every day
Not to let Satan win.

God gives us His grace and power
To forgive the gravest offense.
Everything we need to forgive
He provides with His holy goodness.

Forgiveness is not for the offender.
They may never even know we forgive them.
Forgiveness is for our own peace of mind;
For us to be free again.

Friend do not hold on to offense and pain.
You only hurt yourself.
Let go of all that drags you down
To be free in everything.

I speak to you as one who found
God's love and grace to forgive--
From a heart that was broken and hopeless
To freedom and peace within.

Not to brag for my own glorification,
I did not have the power on my own.
God's grace brought me back from the brink of death
To a life of peace and hope.

Unforgiveness almost killed me.
I prayed to die every day.
I did not understand I was letting myself
Be controlled by the offense and offenders.

I could not forgive on my own
I was too bogged down in grief and pain.
All I wanted was to get even;
To hurt them like I had been hurt.

Satan wanted me miserable and alone.
He thrived on my bitterness and pain.
But I was rescued by God's great love
When He gave me grace to forgive.

God's forgiveness of my own sins
Gave me hope and strength to keep going.
I was set free from Satan's control
When I forgave and gave it to God.

SECTION 8

PSALMS OF PRAYER

Psalm of Prayer for God's Presence

My Lord and my God,
Turn Your Face to me today.
Hear my fervent cry to know
The power of Your presence.

My eyes have been dimmed
By the darkness of the world.
I am struggling to see Your light
In the evil all around me.

My ears are blocked from hearing You
By the roar of hatred everywhere.
The cacophony of the world
Blocks out the sound of Your voice.

I am reaching out to feel
The touch of Your mighty hand.
I am lost without Your guidance
In this foreign land.

l feel that I am sinking
In the raging, roaring sea.
The waves of man's disobedience are
Pulling me down into the deep.

I am struggling to know how to live
In this world of war and strife.
When the evil all around me
Wants to take over all of life.

Weariness of this world
Is troubling my soul.
I feel weak and mortally wounded.
I fear I am losing control.

Lord, I need You more than ever.
Daily I seek You in my need.
I desperately want to know Your will
In all this discontent.

Open my eyes to the beauty of Your presence.
Let me bathe in the pure light of Your grace.
Warm me with the sweetness of Your Spirit.
Let me rest in the comfort of Your love.

Open my ears to hear songs of praise
Being sung to Your Holy name.
In my spirit let me hear Your voice,
Calming the disharmony in my soul.

Let my mind rest in Your Word and
Never doubt Your great power.
Ground me in Your promises
To know You control today and tomorrow.

Help me not to fear the forces of evil,
Nor worry for the future of the ones I love.
Let me dwell in Your peace and stand in Your might
That nothing known to man can destroy.

Let the truth of who You are
Settle deep within my heart.
Give assurance to my soul
That there is nothing You do not control.

Cover me with Your wings.
Banish all fear of evil.
Stir Your presence in my life.
Fill me with your Holy Spirit.

I thank You Lord that I can call
Upon Your Holy name.
In times of trouble and despair,
I know You hear my prayer.

Psalm of Call to Prayer
(We Need to Be on Our Knees)

Evil has overtaken us
In our country that has been blessed.
People have turned away from God.
They think that they know best.

We Christians have let this happen
By being so comfortable.
We have compromised our values
To keep us uninvolved.

We see mass shootings everywhere.
Our hearts are filled with fear.
Hatred for other people
Has left us in despair.

Brutalizing children
Has become a way of life.
Prostitution and sexual sin
Are promoted every day.

We ought to be on our knees
Praying God please spare our country.
We need to be on our knees
Praying God forgive our sins.

We must be on our knees
Praying Lord, we are humbly asking.
Our complacent compromising
Has brought us to this end.

Murder, slaughter, and genocide
Do not bother us anymore.
It is just part of society
We reason within our hearts.

Greed, selfishness, and arrogance,
Are proudly on display.
There is no compassion
For those who have lost their way.

We shake our heads, avert our eyes,
And worry about the future.
But there is no submission
To change it in any way.

Christians we must wake up;
Restore order from decay.
Take a stand and put down our foot
To follow God's Word and way.

We ought to be on our knees
Praying, God, please spare our country.
We need to be on our knees
Praying God, forgive our sins.

We must be on our knees
Praying Lord, we are humbly asking.
Our complacent compromising
Has brought us to this end.

As Christians we are responsible
To turn our country around.
Take the forefront in the fight
To bring back what is right.

Stop the compromising.
Stand up for Christ our Lord.
Do not be afraid to speak His name
In every work and word.

Put on His holy armor.
Get ready for the fight,
He will honor and respond.
He will bring His light.

He will hear our every prayer
When humbleness He sees.
He will not forsake us
When we are on our knees.

We ought to be on our knees
Praying God please spare our country.
We need to be on our knees
Praying God forgive our sins.

We must be on our knees
Praying Lord, we are humbly asking.
Our complacent compromising
Has brought us to this end.

Psalm of Prayer for Forgiveness

Have mercy on me, O God,
For my heart is filled with sin.
The call of this world has enticed me
To fall for Satan's plan.

I strive to live in Your presence,
But my sin keeps me away.
The wickedness within me
Blocks Your countenance from my face.

My heart is full of envy
Of those who have more than I.
The ways of this world around me
Tell me I am not enough.

Thoughts of anger and retribution
Tempting me to hold a grievance
Fill my heart and then my mind
Against all those who have hurt me.

The world tells me to get even
With all those who hurt me in life.
Forgiveness seems an illusion
When the pain is all consuming.

Forgive my thoughts and yearnings
To be the center of attention.
I cannot show the love of Christ
When self-righteousness consumes me.

The pull of earthly gods gets stronger every day.
They constantly tempt and assault me.
Greed, anger, and selfishness
Are things I face daily.

When lust and sexual sin
Fill my mind with evil images,
Bring my heart back to Your presence
In purity and innocence.

This world I live in offers so much to entice me
To turn away from Your truth and goodness.
Give me strength to stand with dignity
From the pull of society's call.

Day after day I am buffeted by sin
To make the wrong choices in life.
Keep me drenched in Your Word, O Lord,
That I will be able to fight.

Father please forgive my sin.
I come to You in repentance.
Have mercy upon me today.
Create a clean heart in me.

Show me how to forgive;
To let go of grievance and pain.
Let me see everyone in the love of the Father,
Even ones who are evil and mean.

Cleanse me with the blood of Jesus,
The one who died for my sins.
Cover me with Your love and Your grace
As I strive on this mortal plain.

You are the only true God.
You deserve worship and praise.
Keep my mind stayed on You only
For all the rest of my days.

Soon I will see You in glory.
I will fall on my face in awe.
Let my soul be clean before You
That I may enter Your glory.

Psalm of Prayer for Intervention (Psalm of a Virus)

Ruler of the universe, Father to us all,
I come today with questions and concerns.
Our whole world is being disrupted
By the presence of a tiny bug.

Our lives are being shaken.
We have not seen this in our time.
People are in a panic.
Fear is running wild.

Things we have taken for granted,
Things we thought would always be there
Are being shuttered and closed away.
Every day there are more and more cases.

Entire countries are begging for help.
Populations are being decimated.
People are going crazy
Not knowing what to expect.

Businesses are closing.
People are losing their jobs.
Supplies are being limited.
Hoarding leaves many without.

We are running out of medical supplies.
We have nothing to fight this illness.
We are fighting over who to blame
Instead of taking precautions.

Children are out of school.
Their parents are distraught.
Suddenly, they must take care of their own.
Many do not know how to manage.

People are taking advantage
Of others not as strong as they.
Many are fighting over toilet paper
While pushing the elderly out of the way.

Selfish, arrogant, and rebellious,
Some refuse to follow the cautions.
They put fun and entertainment
Above anyone else but them.

Each day we hear more bad news.
Every day the death toll rises.
Doctors and nurses are exhausted
Trying to keep patients alive.

Mankind is showing its true heart
In acts of selfishness and fear.
Myriads disregard the danger to others
In a panic to survive.

Our country has believed we are above this.
We are too smart and advanced.
Nothing can bring us to our knees.
We can defeat anything that comes.

Yet, here we are in this mess.
The economy is crashing.
Maybe we are not as smart as we thought.
We are learning a very hard lesson.

Our priorities are confused.
Our goals are polluted.
Society demands our sacrifice
Of things that are so important.

God, are you teaching us a lesson?
Are You giving us another chance?
Is this our last chance to turn back to You
In humbleness and repentance?

Are You showing us how arrogant we are
By allowing us to fail?
Are You waiting to hear us cry to You
By admitting we are weak and frail?

Are You teaching us we need You
As we see so many perish?
When we have nowhere else to go,
You wait patiently to help us.

Are You restoring us to our families
Giving us a chance to see what is vital?
Are you teaching us to play and pray with our children;
To be examples to them?

Dear Father, have mercy on us now.
Take this situation and work it for good.
Let us turn from depending on ourselves
And admit that You hold the solution.

You have told us You hear our prayers;
That You will protect Your children.
Your promise is true if only we will call on You
In times of trouble and peril.

You have said that all who are faithful
Have nothing to fear or dread.
No plague will approach our dwelling[43]
When we put all our trust in You.

God, You are in control of all things.
All things must bow to You.
Nothing can exist without Your permission.
Please eradicate this illness.

Take away this danger,
This virus disrupting our lives.
You are our only help and hope
To make us well again.

We plead for Your mercy and grace.
We cry out for the touch of Your hand.
Free us from this plague we are in
And give us all hope again.

Psalm of Prayer

(Based on the Lord' s Prayer)

O Lord, my God, who resides on Your heavenly throne
Great is Your majesty and grace.
All praise and honor and glory, Lord,
Are ascribed to Your Holy name.

My Savior and Christ, Light of the World,
O Lover of my soul--
I lift my hands in awe of You
And Your holiness and glory.

Let my praise open the door
To Your throne room and Your heart.
I bow before You in adoration and awe.
My life I give to You.

Let Your Kingdom of Light come to my heart.
Let my being reflect Your glory
To all those on earth who need to know
The saving grace You offer.

For I am the emissary of Your love.
I am Your messenger on earth.
Pour Your Holy Spirit into my soul
That I might show Your love.

O Lord, this earth has turned away
From Your presence and Your Word.
Forgive our sins and let Your Kingdom come[44]
On earth as it is in heaven.

Provision You give each day of my life.
Every need is already met.
I thank You for Your mercy and blessing
That daily keep me going.

There are no words to thank You enough
For everything You have already done.
Yet, I ask that You keep me daily supplied
With all I need to sustain me.

My salvation is assured
When I call upon Your name.
You gave up Your life for me.
I am redeemed by the blood of the Lamb.

My sins I lay at Your feet, my Lord.
You have promised to cast them away
As far as the east is from the west.[45]
My guilt is banished this day.

Forgive me, O God, for looking at temptation.
Satan buffets me every day.
I ask for Your strength and power everlasting
To discern him and cast him away.

Give me the same measure of grace that You measure out to me
To forgive all those who have hurt me;
To let go of every grievance and put it away
That I might be forgiven.

I ask for Your hedge of protection
Around all those I love.
Send Your angels to cover them
With the bounty of Your love.

You are Holy Lord.
You rule Your Kingdom in majesty.
Your glory shines forth in heavenly splendor
As angels praise Your name.

Forever and ever You will reign.
There is no God but You.
I fall to my knees and lift my hands
To give honor to Your Name.

To my Lord, my God, My Savior, and King,
Yours is the power and the glory.
Amen and amen forever more,
And again, I say amen.

Psalm of Prayer for Salvation

Jesus my Savior, I come.
I come with a heart heavy with sin.
I bring all the dirty rags of my life
To the one who can cleanse me within.

My life has been one of misery--
Living each day on my own.
Trying to make a success of my life,
Has left me empty and unfulfilled.

I know I have sinned often and greatly
With so many, many sins against You.
Evil invaded my heart and my mind,
Leaving me in darkness.

My soul is empty and hard.
I have never given You a thought.
I believed only in myself
To make sense of the life I sought.

Now I know of Your great love;
How You gave Your life for my sins.
I do not understand this great mercy,
But I know in my heart it is real.

Jesus, forgive my transgressions.
Take this heart and make it brand new.
I give you everything that I am.
I give my heart and soul to You.

I thank You Lord for this gift
That You freely and lovingly give.
From this moment I know I am forgiven.
I accept Your mercy and love.

I am freed from the sins that plagued me.
I have never felt so alive.
You filled my heart with Your love.
My soul is now clean and pure.

Show me how to know You.
Be my constant companion and friend.
May my life now reflect Your glory
Until my days shall come to an end.

Psalm of Prayer on Maundy Thursday

My Heavenly Father, Savior, and Lord,
I am so keenly aware of my sin.
On this eve of Your crucifixion,
My mind goes to Your suffering.

As You went to the Mount of Olives
To cry out to Your Father on high.
I was one of those who was with You;
Sleeping while You agonized.

When the soldiers came to arrest You,
Led by one of Your own in betrayal,
I was afraid to speak out for You.
I cringed in fear at the sight.

As You stood before priests and governors,
I was part of the unruly crowd.
I shouted out my denial
Of knowing who You were.

I was one of the angry throngs,
Who, in hatred, cried out for Your death.
The rabble who turned against You
Shouted out "Crucify."

In belief that my actions were justified,
I placed the crown of thorns upon Your head.
Then I lifted the cross onto Your back
And followed with mocking and scorn.

I held the nails as they were hammered
Into Your hands and Your feet.
I lifted You up for all to see
As my own sins crashed down on Your head.

My hand thrust the sword in Your side
As You hung there dying for me.
My eyes took in Your suffering
As You cried out "Father forgive."

Every one of my sins You carried
Just as if I were standing right there.
The sins of the world You took
On Your human body so frail.

Lord Jesus, You died in agony
That I might have eternal life.
You went to the grave all alone,
Rising again to save me from death.

Cleanse me Lord, with Your blood,
The blood You poured out for me.
Take my sins and cast them away
As You did at Calvary.

Forgive me, Savior, when I fail You,
When I betray You and turn away.
Forgive me when I refuse to love others,
As You loved me when You hung there that day.

Lord Jesus, forgive me again today
Just as You did long ago.
Take my guilt and regret away
And wash me white as snow.

SECTION 9

PSALMS OF WARNING

Psalm for the USA

The enemy is at the gates of our land.
Devastation and destruction are coming.
The great sin that has encompassed us
Is tearing our land to pieces.

We look at our country with fear.
Our hearts are sinking within us.
The division of hatred and anger
Is carrying us away to our doom.

People are fighting with each other
With no reason other than hate.
We are torn apart by differing beliefs.
We refuse to cease our resentment.

There are many enemies already among us.
Evil is rampant in its disguise.
Enemies plot to destroy us
By dividing us from within.

Our government on which we stand
Is being torn asunder by hate.
Officials sworn to protect us
Can only think of themselves.

Debauchery and destructive behavior
Have a strong hold on society.
Murder has become so common place.
Our hearts have been hardened and cannot see it.

Laws made for our protection
Are broken in heinous ways.
Every day we hear cries against them.
"They are suppressing our freedom," people say.

Love, understanding, and forgiveness are almost non-existent.
They are no longer politically correct.
Respect, cooperation, and reconciliation
Are considered as weaknesses in our times.

Babies are ripped apart in abortion.
There is no respect for life.
Nothing is considered wrong
If justified by convenience.

The United States of America has stood for over 200 years.
We have been staid in our faith and belief.
God has given us power and wealth beyond measure.
No other country has been so blessed.

Our forefathers knew, so long ago,
For us to become a country of prestige,
We must adhere to the laws of God.
It is written in our Constitution.

The many blessings and freedoms given by God
Are now being misused and undermined.
They have for so long been taken for granted.
People ignore them with no expectation of accountability.

Other countries sit back in laughter at our ignorance and defiance.
They are delightfully seeing their goals realized.
We are destroying ourselves from within.
They are just waiting on our demise.

People of God, we must rise up
Against the dangers and evil overtaking us.
Compromise has been our enemy
And complacency our downfall.

We must fall on our knees in prayer;
Humble ourselves before God.
Plead for His forgiveness
For healing and for restoration.

God in heaven, Almighty Father,
We have turned from You and Your law.
You are giving us warning after warning.
Yet, we continue to seek after wrong.

Father, look on our land with mercy.
Forgive our grievous sins.
Let us humble ourselves before You
To plead for our country again.

Grant us freedom to live and freedom to worship
Your awesome name, O God.
Bless us with freedom from fear and terror
From others who would destroy us.

We must turn our hearts to You, Lord;
Turn away from the evil that besets us.
Spare us from captivity and destruction.
Return our country to prosperity.

Psalm of Warning

People of Christ look up!
The end time is upon us.
The prophets foretold for many ages
The signs and warnings of His coming.

People of the earth look up
For the signs that are all around.
The devil is moving quickly
To deceive and lead us astray.

Many things foretold in the Scriptures are occurring every day.
Many are not looking and will fail to see.
Our world has turned from its Maker,
And His judgment will not long be contained.

As in the days of Noah,
The world has embraced so much evil.
As in the days of Sodom and Gomorrah,
Sin is rampant and on display.

Evil ones cry over the abuse of a puppy,
Then rejoice at the tearing apart of a baby.
Nature is more esteemed
Then the life of an innocent child.

People cry to save the trees
But want to get rid of the elderly.
They want to save the animals
But desert the poor and deprived.

Children and youth are being deceived
Into lives of drugs and enslaved to prostitution.
These innocents are being used
As tools of greed and avarice.

We see signs of earthquakes and floods,
Tornadoes, and disruptions of the weather.
Hurricanes and storms are more violent than ever.
God is giving us warning after warning.

Attempts to explain away these events
Such as global warming and pollution
Are in direct contradiction
To how God describes the last days.

Knowledge and advancement on intellectual levels
Have given people a sense of control.
We now look to the intellect of man
Instead of the pure Word of God.

The degradation of society and the extremes in moral decay
Have reached heights of arrogance and pride never seen before today.
The world has given men the right, in all its knowledge and sin,
To determine their own morality and not obey the Lord's command.

We are lovers of self, lovers of money, proud, and arrogant people.
Ungratefulness, unholiness, and heartlessness are sins of the devil's work.
People have become more hate-filled and brutal than ever before--
A sure sign of departure from God.

Nations rise against nations
In more violent ways than before.
Each nation is developing weapons
Of total annihilation.

Every day more tensions and fears
Are surrounding the nations of earth.
Superpowers of the world are making ready
For a war to end all wars.

People continue to look for fulfillment,
But in arrogance and pride refuse to see the truth.
False prophets are taking advantage of sin;
Telling us Scripture must change with the culture.

Disobedience is rampant.
People, swollen with deceit, declare "There is no God."
Evil prowls the earth like a lion stalking its prey,
Deceiving even God's people to look away.

The powerful pull of the gods of this world
Is leading us into its trap.
God has spoken in His first command,
There shall be no gods before Me.

The destruction of God's own people, so many times before,
Was caused by the people turning away from God.
Over and over, God called them to come back,
Bur their arrogance and disobedience led to their destruction.

Child sacrifice, disrespect for life, and lifestyles abhorrent to God
Were put on display with evil delight.
The worship of gods, who demanded deprivation,
Led to the annihilation of the people who served them.

Look up world, turn away from Your sin.
God's tolerance will not last much longer.
The only hope for our world today
Is to turn back to God and repent.

He lovingly waits for all people to come
To the realization of His salvation.
Turn away from your arrogance, selfishness, and pride,
To the wonder and beauty in Him.

O world without guidance, without peace, without hope,
Turn to the only One who can save us.
He is the way, the truth, and the light.
He is giving us one last chance.

We must turn away from the idols of this world.
We must value all life as holy.
We must turn to God in humbleness.
We must ask for forgiveness from our sins.

Psalm of Darkness and Light

Each of us has a choice to make
As we go through our daily existence.
We live on this plane of mortal life
Between two dimensions of darkness and light.

The Kingdom of God is the way of light.
He opens the door for our peace and joy.
The realm of Satan contains the darkness
That pulls us toward judgment and fear.

Each year, every hour, and every second
We choose to see darkness or light.
The choice determines how our life is lived
In victory or utter defeat.

God gives us the light of His love
In forgiveness, peace, and hope.
There is no fear in His love:[46]
No judgment, no grievance, no doubt.

The darkness holds fear in everything and
Fear of losing all that we have.
It causes us to live in grievance, blame,
Guilt, ego, and pride.

In true love there are no expectations.
Unconditional love forgives.
It holds no record of grievance or wrong
It lets go of all hurt and pain.

We live in anxiety, loneliness, and guilt
When we let darkness rule our mind.
The absence of peace, love, and faith in God
Leaves us hopeless and full of desire.

Light gives us a stronghold to run to
When troubles attack our life.
It gives us hope in a world full of strife
When all we can see is wrong.

Judgment of others causes us to be judged.
When we do not forgive, we are not forgiven.
Grievances we hold can cause us to murder
In our thoughts, in our words, and in our deeds.

Unmet expectations cause anger and hurt.
They destroy the old and the young.
Ego and pride in who we are on our own
Bring sorrow and anguish to many.

We are conditioned to live in darkness
By a world that has forgotten the light.
The poison of evil has darkened our minds
Against all that is holy and good.

Experiencing God and His kingdom of light
Is what gives us the power to know
We can overcome the old mind of darkness
And live in the new mind of Christ.

In light we can love and forgive and exist
In a brand-new world of peace.
The presence of God will light our way
To the brightest tomorrow today.

Psalm of Sorrow

Innocent blood cries out from the ground
Reaching the Father's ears with deafening sound.
Blood poured out by sin and degradation
At the hand of His own creation.

Little ones, precious gifts of the Father,
Are being slaughtered for convenience.
They lose their lives that were woven by God
At the whim of another.

Oh Lord, how Your heart must break
As You see the selfishness of those You created.
Disregard for lives so holy
Must bring You sorrow one cannot measure.

The world has turned away from You.
It thinks nothing of slaughter and murder.
Hearts have become so calloused and hard
By raising themselves above You.

How can life continue
With so much greed and hate?
These beautiful blessings You give us
Are being treated with disdain.

Unbelief around us rages.
Your Word is disregarded.
People doubt Your truth and Your power.
They flaunt their rejection of You.

Lord, we perish in our rejection.
We perish with so much pride.
We have forgotten that You can save us and
That You love us beyond all measure.

As innocent blood flows out before You,
God, take it and make it holy.
Wash it with Your tears of grief,
And sanctify it to Yourself.

For there was another time when blood was shed by man.
It, too, was shed by the hand of arrogance and pride.
But the blood of Jesus was willingly given
That we might be free from our sin.

The blood of Jesus running down from His body
Spread drops of grief on the ground.
As its cry lifted up to the heavens,
The Father heard, and He granted its plea.

"Father, forgive them," He cried in His suffering[47]
As His crimson blood dropped slowly to the ground.
First a cry, then a whisper, as His life ebbed away.
That holy blood is still crying today.

It is crying for our salvation
From the evil that besets us.
It cries for the lost and forsaken
In this world that has lost its first love.

The blood You shed to save us
Can restore our righteousness.
When we fall on our knees to plead for mercy,
Bring us to Your bleeding side.

We cry for the lives of Your children,
Who are being torn apart and cast aside.
They are the ones who are given no chance to live
By the evil of selfish ambition.

Lord, we plead for Your forgiveness.
Forgive our apostacy.
Let the blood You gave to save us
Cleanse our hearts and make us free.

Psalm of the Gods of this World

The gods of this world
Are prowling and stalking.
They are after the spirits
Of every person on earth.

Satan's minions have only one mission--
To seek, to inhabit, and to destroy.
Their goal is to fill up Satan's living hell
With the souls they control until death.

Many and varied are these gods.
Some are not what we expect.
They use their cunning to take control
And put the true God out of mind.

These gods are masters of masquerade.
They do not want to appear as evil.
Their desire is to make folks so comfortable that
We do not realize what we are doing.

Some are worse than others in our minds.
We have made allowances for ourselves.
Yet, anything that takes our attention from God
Is a false and evil companion.

Most everyone admits that violence and murder
Are evils of the vilest imaginings.
Children are kidnapped and abused every day
For pornography, slavery, and prostitution.

These evils are so horrendous that
Most people shudder to see them.
Yet, they grew from lesser evils
Invited into the souls of people.

Things we do not think of as evil
We allow readily into our lives.
Selfishness, greed, disrespect, and rebellion
Can grow into the height of evil.

The god of self has taken control.
We need to seek society's approval.
Caught up in the delusion of who we should be,
We deny our true worth in God.

Body worship, beauty, vanity, and pride
Take our eyes off who we were created to be
No matter the cost one must pay,
We change ourselves to the standards of today.

Narcissism, anxiety, and worry
Take over our mind and body.
We fail to depend on the wisdom of God and
Replace it with things we cannot control.

Money and success are the great motivators.
We are willing to do whatever it takes to get them.
Dishonesty, greed, and selfishness
Become acceptable if it gets us more money.

Possessions mean more than anything.
We must have more and more all the time.
We spend money we do not have
To keep up with the current trend.

Additive behaviors look so promising
To make us happy and fill our souls.
As we open our lives to their influence,
They become so strong they take all control.

Drunkenness, drugs, smoking, and harmful substances
Become stronger and stronger until we are addicted.
They are using our bodies to lead to slow death.
They are laughing as we kill ourselves.

Social media, entertainment, and amusements
Seem an innocent way to have fun.
But the images we let into our minds from these things
Become manifest in us the longer we see them.

Even food and health can become false gods
When we use them inappropriately.
They become the focus of our every thought,
Allowing vanity and gluttony to take over.

The false god of disrespect,
Has become so prevalent today.
Hatefulness and disobedience abound.
There is no accountability for actions.

Hatred exists for anyone
Who does not agree with our beliefs.
Hate always causes division and lawlessness
And ultimately takes control of our actions.

Pride is a god who seeks attention.
It makes us see ourselves better than we are.
It creates a sense of entitlement.
Self becomes the only thing that matters.

There are so many other false gods of earth
That will creep unwittingly into our lives.
Often, we do not even realize
We are giving them control over us.

Anything that takes our eyes off God
And pulls our lives and thoughts into it
Becomes a lesser god in our lives
Until it totally blinds us.

The only thing we can be sure of
Is that there is only one true God.
He is the God who commands our love
And all our devotion to Him.

Yet, He will never force us
To look away from the things of earth.
We each must choose which gods we serve.
We are given that free will.

The gods of this world will never stop.
They grow stronger and more controlling as we let them.
They know that they are ultimately defeated
By the sacrifice of Jesus.

So, choose this day which god you will serve[48]
For you cannot worship both God and self.
There is a way that seems right to man,
But in the end, it leads to destruction.

We must keep our eyes on the God of all;
Not give in to the wiles of evil.
We must stand in strength against Satan's call
And not give our souls to hell.

Psalm of Heaven and Hell

I cannot imagine how people can live
Without God's saving love.
To contemplate death as final
Is beyond my understanding.

God's own Word tells us plainly
There is a heaven and hell:
Heaven, for those who accept Him;
Hell, for those who reject Him.

Heaven and hell are both described.
God's Word gives us clear descriptions.
Having this knowledge available to us
Gives us every opportunity to choose.

Heaven will be such a glorious place with
Streets of gold, gates of pearl, and contentment.
It will be a home forever and ever to praise
The great God our Holy King.

There will be no sorrow there;
No crying or sickness or pain.
Our bodies will be a reflection
Of our maker in all His glory.

There we will see our loved ones,
Who have died and gone before us.
There will be a wonderful reunion with those we loved and lost--
The ones who shaped our lives for this glory.

There will be no more darkness or confusion
About the trials of life.
No more hatred, anger, or malice will exist.
Peace and joy will reign supremely.

Our Holy God will be in our midst
Surrounded by His angels.
The brightness that covers us through Him
Brings glory to our heavenly being.

Hell, the place of great sadness, is
Satan's kingdom of destruction.
Those who have rejected the Savior
Will be tortured forever and ever.

Satan, the mouthpiece of hell,
Is determined to fill up his kingdom,
He prowls around like a roaring lion
Devouring all who let him.

Chains of blackest darkness will bind all inhabitants there.
The burning of flesh in agony will never ever be ended.
They will thirst and cry out for water,
But their thirst will never be quenched.

Hatred, anger, pain, and despair
Will be the only emotions there.
Knowledge of where they could have been
Will haunt them forever and ever.

Woe to those who reject Jesus;
Who turn to evil temptations.
Those who proclaim, "There is no God"
Will be cast into the lake of fire.

Dear friends, I plead for your life
That you may join me in heaven.
Accept Jesus as your Lord and Savior
With open arms He will welcome you in.

Your sins will be forgiven
No matter how grievous or evil.
He will cast them as far as the east from the west.
You will be cleansed and set free by His blood.

He will prepare for you a home.
In His beautiful kingdom of heaven.
Everlasting life in His presence
Will be your ultimate reward.

I will not fear or worry
For heaven will be my home.
God's love and forgiveness
Have prepared a place for me there.

SECTION 10

PSALMS OF VICTORY

Psalm of Jesus's Return

I look to the skies and long for the day
When the heavens will be split open.
Jesus will descend from the clouds,
And I will be going home.

Oh, what a wondrous day that will be
When all His glory we shall see.
The trumpets will sound to announce His presence,
And His angels will cover the sky.

The dead in Christ will rise from their graves
As they shout in victory.
Then those who know Him and remain alive[49]
Will meet Him in the air.

All those who have rejected Him
Will fall on their knees in fear.
Their empty spirits will cry out
In horror as they realize who they are.

People will raise their arms
And cry out to be included.
They realize too late
Their unbelief has doomed them.

There will be weeping and screams of fear
By those who are left behind.
Satan will be unleashed
To completely destroy mankind.

Mothers will cry for their children
As they rise to meet the Lord.
Spouses will cry out for mates,
Who have prayed for them for years.

Families will be split apart--
Some rising, some left behind.
The grief of those who remain
Will be a testament of those refusing the Word.

The world will be in chaos.
Everything will be disrupted.
There will be a collapse of all that was before
Built by the arrogance of man.

Darkness will fall upon the earth--
The darkness of sin and evil.
There will be no peace or comfort
For those who denied His name.

There will be looting and murder.
People will turn on each other.
All that gave happiness will be destroyed
As Satan takes over each person.

People will run for cover
As their homes will no longer be safe.
No laws or rules will be followed.
Each one is left to his own.

There will no hiding places
From the evil that will reign.
The streets will become like battlefields
Where killing is done for pleasure.

Satan will unleash his demons
To destroy all things completely,
He will be laughing and declaring his ownership
Of all people left on the earth.

No punishment known to man
Will be as bad as what will come.
The wrath of all the evil ones
Will torture each mind and body.

Yet, God's people, who have risen,
Will be shouting praises to Him.
They will live in joy and peace
In an eternity of love.

I hope to see you there
As we rise with the Lord of all.
Turn from the ways of the world
And give your life to God.

Psalm of Release

Father, my body is weary and worn.
I am longing for heaven and home.
This frail body of earth has run its race
I am ready to collect my reward.

You have appointed to man a set number of days.
This earthly body cannot last forever.
The days You give are full of work and strife
That wear down our constitution.

This body was not intended to be my eternal abode.
This earth is not my final home.
When I give heart and soul to You,
My life is insured forever.

God, I am impatient to be in Your perfect glory, and
To see You seated on Your throne.
I will fall on my knees and shout, "holy"
To the one who welcomes me home.

Death is not my conqueror.
Christ sealed that fate long ago.
Death only opens the door
To my eternal home.

Lord, I am ready to behold You;
To look on Your glorious face.
I am ready to leave all this world behind and
To dwell in Your holy place.

I will close the eyes of this earthly shell.
It will cease to breath and function.
Then to beauty and majesty I shall arise
To the open arms of Jesus.

Psalm to Death

Death, I do not fear you.
You are only another part of life.
My ultimate end does not rest in you.
You have been conquered by Jesus the Christ.

This body will wear out.
It will decay and return to dust.
Yet, I will be alive and well and
Dwelling with God in His home.

From illness, fatigue, and stress,
I will ultimately be set free.
A perfect new body of glory
In heaven is waiting for me.

Death, you are not the victor.
Over me you have no hold.
I am not bound in your chilling grasp.
You are only a vehicle to my reward.

My Jesus has freed me from your control
With His death and resurrection.
You have no power or dominion over me
Because He defeated you forever.

Children of Christ have no dread of you.
We know death is not our end.
We will be even more alive
When we see our God in heaven.

So, death I do not fear you.
Never will you distress me.
I will not live in dread of you
Nor tremble at your inevitability.

I will not contemplate my demise.
I will not waste my time in fright.
But I will rejoice when I think of you,
You open my way to eternal life.

A Psalm for the Church in the Modern Age

Church of God stand fast, stand strong
For you are the bride of Christ.
You were established upon the Rock of the Lord.
He is your foundation everlasting.

The head of the church is Christ our Lord.
It is nourished and cherished by Him.
We stand on the truth of His inerrant Word;
Not of our own knowledge and wisdom.

The church has stood for thousands of years
Through storm, through strife, through war.
Strengthened by His Love and His Hand,
The church perseveres by His Word.

In His Word God tells us to expect persecution[50]
But to fear no evil nor madness.
He is the mighty stronghold of faith
Upon which the church stands proudly.

The church stands fast and holds to our doctrine--
Not of man but of the commands of God.
Established by Him and built by His people,
Holy and glorified, it will be presented to God.

Love the Lord your God with all your heart[51]
Is the first command to the church.
"Love others with that same love," He says.
The second is like to the first.

To follow Christ in the way of His love
Is to love even those who are evil.
That is the mission God gives to His church
To keep to the day of His coming.

Evil is trying to destroy the church
By any way or means it can conjure.
Satan's goal is to overthrow, to kill, and then to plunder,
While blinding man to the promise of Christ.

Violence comes from the mouth of the wicked.[52] We see it every day.
Evil is like sport to the fool[53] as it was in Solomon's day.
False prophets will come to distort His Word;
To be imitators of Christ's true church.

God tells the church not to be afraid.
Do not fret as it only causes harm.
Do not let anger block out sight of our Christ.
But speak wisdom, peace, and love.

Persevere, be strong, overcome with love.
Do not enter the path of the wicked.
The gods of this age have blinded the many
To the truth God plainly gives us.

To all the principalities and powers of this age
The church must make known God's wisdom.
To those who would destroy the upright of the Lord
We must stand on the boldness of Christ.

God will not allow His church to be destroyed
As He did with the church of the Baals.
His people must stand on the Rock of His truth
In our speech, in our love, and in our faith.

Stand firm, O Church, on the Word of the Lord.
Do everything to perfect the gospel of peace.
He will not forsake those established in Him.
His church will stand strong through the ages.

End Notes

1   He was despised and rejected by men, A Man of Sorrows an acquainted with grief. Isaiah 14:6 (NKJ)

2   Jesus said to him, "I am the way, the truth and the life; No man cometh to the Father, but by Me." John 14:6 (NKJ)

3   Great is the Lord and greatly to be praised Rejoice always, and His greatness is unsearchable. Psalm 145:3 (ESV)

4   God said to Moses, "I AM WHO I AM." Tell the people of Israel I AM sent me to you. Exodus 3:14 (MSV)

5   Who is the King of Glory? The Lord strong and mighty, The Lord mighty in battle. Psalm 24:8 (NKJ)

6   God said to Moses, "I AM WHO I AM." Tell the people of Israel I AM sent me to you. Exodus 3:14 (MSV)

7   That at the name of Jesus every knee shall bow, of those in heaven and those on the earth, and those under the earth. Philippians 2:10 (NKJ)

8   He counts the stars; He calls them by name. Psalm 147:4 (NKJ)

9   The heavens declare the glory of God; and the skies proclaim the works of His hand. Psalm 19:1 (NIV)

10   Bless the Lord O my soul, and all that is within me bless His Holy Name. Bless the Lord O my soul and forget not all His benefits. Psalm 103:1-2 (NKJ)

11   He was despised and rejected by men, A Man of Sorrows and acquainted with grief. And we hid, as it were, our faces from Him. Isaiah 53:3 (NKJ)

12   Then Jesus said, "Father forgive them for they do not know what they do." And they divided His garments and cast lots. Luke 23:24 (NKJ)

13   Now when the Sabbath was past, Mary Magdalene, Mary, the mother of James, and Salome brought spices that they might come and anoint His body. Mark 16:1 (NKJ)

14   God said to Moses, "I AM WHO I AM." Tell the people of Israel I AM sent me to you. Exodus 3:14 (MSV)

15   Love is patient, love is kind, it does not envy, it does not boast, it is not proud. It does not dishonor others, it is not self-seeking, it is not easily angered, it keeps no record of wrong. Love does not delight in evil but rejoices with the truth. It

always protects, always trusts, always hopes, always perseveres. 1 Corinthians 13:4-7 (NIV)

16 For You created my innermost being, You knit me together in my mother's womb. Psalm 139:13 (NKJ)

17 I praise You because I am fearfully and wonderfully made; Marvelous are Your works and that my soul knows full well. Psalm 139:14 (NKJ)

18 See that you do not despise one of these little ones. For I tell you that in heaven their angels always see the face of my Father who is in heaven. Matthew 18:10 (ESV)

19 God is our refuge and strength. A very present help in trouble. Psalm 46:1 (NKJ)

20 I praise You because I am fearfully and wonderfully made; Marvelous are Your works and that my soul knows full well. Psalm 139:14 (NKJ)

21 For we do not wrestle against flesh and blood, but against principalities and powers. Against spiritual hosts of wickedness in the Heavenly places. Ephesians 6:12 (NKJ)

22 Rejoice always, pray without ceasing. 1 Thessalonians 5:16-17 (NKJ)

23 Thy Word is a lamp unto my feet and a light unto my path. Psalm 199:105 (NKJ)

24 For the Word of God is living and powerful and sharper than any two-edged sword, piercing even the division of the soul and spirit; and joints and marrow, and is the discerner of the thoughts and intentions of the heart. Hebrews 4:12 (NKJ)

25 The Lord has appeared of old to me saying, "Yes I have loved you with and everlasting love; therefore, with loving kindness I have drawn you." Jeremiah 31:3 (NKJ)

26 Many waters cannot quench love, nor can the floods drown it. If a man would give for love all the wealth of his house, it would utterly be condemned. Song of Solomon 8:7 (NKJ)

27 What is man that You are mindful of him, and the son of man that you visit him. Psalm 8:4 (NKJ)

28 You have made him a little lower than the angels, You have crowned him with glory and honor, and set him over the works of Your hands. Hebrews 2:7 (NKJ)

29 There is no fear in love. But perfect love drives out fear because fear has to do with punishment. The one who fears is not made of perfect love. 1 John 4:8 (NIV)

30 Since his days are determined, the number of his months is with you. You have appointed his limits so that he cannot pass. Job 14:5 (NKJ)

31 Trust in the Lord with all your heart and lean not on your own understanding. Proverbs 3:5 (NKJ)

32 Jesus said to him, "I am the way, the truth and the life. No one comes to the Father except by Me." John 14:6 (NKJ)

33 For God so loved the world that He gave His only begotten Son, that whosoever believes in Him, should not perish but have everlasting life. John 3:16 (KJV)

34 He has shown you O man, what is good; and what does the Lord require of you but to do justly, to love mercy, and to walk humbly with your God. Micah 6:8 (NKJ)

35 Whom having not seen Your love, though now you do not see Him, yet believing, you rejoice with inexpressible joy and full of glory. 1 Peter 1:8 (NKJ)

36 And the peace of God, which surpasses all understanding will guard your hearts and minds through Christ Jesus. Philippians 4:7 (NKJ)

37 Jesus said to him, "You shall love the Lord your God with all your heart, with all your soul, and with all your mind. This is the first commandment and the second is like it; you shall love your neighbor as yourself." Matthew 22:37-39 (NKJ)

38 These things I have spoken to you that in Me you might have peace. In the world you will have tribulation but be of good cheer. I have overcome the world. John 27:33 (NKJ)

39 There is a way that seems right to man, but its end is the way of death. Proverbs 14:12 (NKJ)

40 Do not enter the way of the wicked, and do not walk in the way of evil. Proverbs 4:14 (NKJ)

41 Jesus said to him, "I do not say up to seven times, but up to seventy times seven." Matthew 18:22 (KJV)

42 Then Jesus said, "Father forgive them for they do not know what they do." And they divided His garments and cast lots. Luke 23:24 (NKJ)

43 No evil shall befall you, nor shall any plague come near your dwelling. Psalm 91:15 (NKJ)

44 Your kingdom come; Your will be done on earth as it is in heaven. Matthew 6:10 (KJV)

45 As far as the east is from the west, so far, He has removed our transgressions from us. Psalm 103:2 (NKJ)

46 There is no fear in love. But perfect love drives out fear; because fear has to do with punishment. The one who fears is not made in perfect love. 1 John 4:18 (NKJ)

47 Then Jesus said, "Father forgive them for they do not know what they are doing." And they divided His garments and cast lots. Luke 24:30 (NKJ)

48 And if it seems evil to you to serve the Lord, choose for yourself, this day, whom you will serve, whether the gods which your fathers served on the other side of the river, or the gods of the Amorites in whose land you dwell. But as for me and my house, we will serve the Lord. Joshua 24:15 (NKJ)

49 For the Lord will descend with a shout, and with the voice of an archangel, and with the trumpet of God. And the dead in Christ will rise first. Then we who

are alive and remain will be caught up together with them in the clouds to meet the Lord in the air, and thus we shall always be with the Lord. 1 Thessalonians 4:16-17 (NKJ)

50 In fact, everyone who wants to live a godly life in Christ Jesus will be persecuted. 2 Timothy 3:12 (NKJ)

51 Jesus said to him, "You shall love the Lord your God with all your heart, with all your soul, and with all your mind. This is the first commandment." Matthew 23:37 (NKJ)

52 Blessings crown the head of the righteous, but violence comes from the mouth of the wicked. Proverbs 10:6 (NIV)

53 To do evil is like sport to a fool. But a man of understanding has wisdom. Proverbs 10:23 (NKJ)

Printed in the United States
By Bookmasters